SUMMER SMARTS

Jeanne Crane Castafero and Janet van Roden

Houghton Mifflin Company
New Ways to Know®

D1451240

Dear Parents,

What is the purpose of Summer Smarts?

Summer Smarts is a summer workbook that enables your child to review knowledge and reinforce skills learned in third grade. The intent of Summer Smarts is not to teach but to provide a bridge between third and fourth grades.

How does Summer Smarts differ from other workbooks?

Summer Smarts contains a unique integration of material, combining the traditional grade school subject matter into one workbook. Summer Smarts is a concise, direct way for your child to review the grade she or he has just completed. The instructions are to the point. Although the material is fun and often surprising, it always is sensible material with a point.

How should Summer Smarts be used?

The worksheets in Summer Smarts are arranged in logical sequence, moving from easier concepts to harder ones. In order to take advantage of the sequencing and integration, we suggest that the workbook be done in order.

The reading books are an integral part of Summer Smarts. Although the worksheets for the reading books are found at the end of Summer Smarts, we encourage your child to space the reading books throughout the summer and not save them until the end.

What sort of reading books are used in Summer Smarts?

A lot of care has been taken in choosing the books used in our reading section. Since pre-fourth graders vary greatly in their reading ability, we have also provided a section where your child may choose his or her own book. If the books we have chosen are generally easy for your child, use the free selections to increase the level of difficulty. On the other hand, if the books we have chosen are generally too challenging, use the free selections to decrease difficulty.

Please keep in mind the obvious: children are incredibly different! We do not want your child to dread Summer Smarts. Use discretion about the pace at which you use this workbook and even about how much of the workbook your child completes.

There is an answer key located at the end of this book to assist you and your child.

Have a great—and smart—summer!

Sincerely,

Jeanne   *Janet*

Jeanne Crane Castafero and Janet van Roden

Contents

BOOK SECTION

Who Are You?

Who are you? When you are with your friends, you may act differently than you act when you are with your family. When you are in the classroom, you may act a third way. People who know you might describe you differently. Who are you?

caring	sneaky	lazy	funny	fast	sad
serious	loving	beautiful	bored	critical	honest
busy	kind	strong	creative	cruel	slow
lonely	wild	sensitive	wise	noisy	sensible

1. What 3 adjectives might your mom use to describe you? Use adjectives from the list above or choose your own.

   _____   _____   _____

2. What 3 adjectives might your friends use to describe you?

   _____   _____   _____

3. What 3 adjectives might your teachers use to describe you?

   _____   _____   _____

4. Did you choose different adjectives for your mom, your friends, and your teachers? Why do you think that people might describe you differently?

   _____

   _____

   _____

   _____

   _____

1

5. What 3 adjectives would *you* use to describe *yourself*? Use these adjectives in at least 3 complete sentences to tell who you really are—because <u>who</u> knows <u>you</u> better than <u>you</u>?

_____

_____

_____

_____

_____

_____

_____

_____

In the box below, draw or paste a picture of something you are doing this summer. Write a caption for it.

_____

_____

WHeRe DO YOU LiVE?

Once upon a time there lived a _____ on a street named
                                        girl or boy?

_____. The street was found in the city or town called
name your street

_____ in the county of _____
name your city or town   **name your county**

and the state named _____. That state was found in the
                         name your state

country named _____. The country was found on the
                    name your country

continent of _____, which was in
                   name your continent

the _____ hemisphere. The hemisphere was
         northern or southern?

on the planet called _____, in the galaxy known
                           name your planet

as _____. So, now do you know
         name your galaxy

where _____ lived?
            write your full name here

Traveling

Answer these questions about where you live.

1. Is **your state** above or below the equator? _____

2. Is **your school** closer to Europe or South America? _____

3. Is **your city** in the northeast, northwest, southeast, southwest, or central part of **your state**? _____

4. Is **your state** in the northeast, northwest, southeast, southwest, or central part of the United States? _____

5. Which ocean is closest to **your state**? _____

6. Which mountain range is closest to **your city**? _____

7. Which major river is closest to **your home**? _____

8. Do you live on a star or a planet? _____

9. Was **your state** one of the original states? _____

10. Name a state that you have visited: _____ Is that state north, south, east, or west of **your state**? _____

11. Is the state you have listed above larger or smaller than **your state**?

    _____

12. Name a city that you have visited: _____ Is that city larger or smaller than **your city**? _____

Read About It

Mr. Popper does quite a bit of traveling with his entourage of penguins in *Mr. Popper's Penguins* by Richard and Florence Atwater.

Show Me Your Math

In each section, examples are done for you.

Write in standard form.

9000 + 6000 = 15,000

1. eight hundred sixteen = _____
2. 5000 + 400 + 6 = _____
3. 6000 + 40 + 2 = _____
4. six thousand one = _____
5. two thousand six = _____

What is halfway between?

60, 70 = 65

1. 1000, 2000 = _____
2. 350, 360 = _____
3. 8000, 9000 = _____
4. 40, 50 = _____
5. 200, 300 = _____

Write in words.

9010 = nine thousand ten

1. 220 = _____
2. 1067 = _____
3. 7777 = _____
4. 601 = _____
5. 8496 = _____

Write the value of the 8.

9680 = 80

1. 8043 = _____
2. 7238 = _____
3. 9853 = _____

Write the correct Roman numeral.

10 = X

1. 5 = _____
2. 4 = _____
3. 9 = _____
4. 25 = _____
5. 39 = _____
6. 17 = _____

Write the value of 4.

407 = 400

1. 642 = _____
2. 43,597 = _____
3. 49 = _____
4. 8472 = _____

Write the correct number.

XXXV = 35

1. VIII = _____
2. XXXIV = _____
3. XIX = _____
4. XXVII = _____

Put these numbers in order from smallest to largest.

34,546   99   887   300,000   6987

_____

_____

_____

Solve this word problem.

Ashley has 12 pieces of candy. Derek has 4 pieces of candy. Sam has 8 pieces of candy. If Mom said that all the children had to have the SAME amount of candy, how many pieces would each child get?

_____

Ski Sentences

In numbers 1 through 7 below, first mark either <u>S</u> if the words make a complete sentence or <u>F</u> if the words are a fragment.

Then, go back to the <u>sentences</u> and put capital letters, periods, and question marks where they belong.

Finally, add words and punctuation to the <u>fragments</u> to make them complete sentences.

EXAMPLE: <u>S</u>   a man rode the chair lift

Corrected: A man rode the chair lift.

  <u>F</u>   a broken ski

Corrected: I was sold a broken ski.

1. _____ went down all the easy hills

   Corrected: _____

2. _____ in every snack bar

   Corrected: _____

3. _____ lauren never fell all day

   Corrected: _____

4. _____ ski slopes are most crowded on holidays

   Corrected: _____

5. _____ not allowed down the hardest slopes

   Corrected: _____

6. _____ under the ski lift

   Corrected: _____

7. _____ my brother won the ski race

   Corrected: _____

Each group of words is two sentences. Separate the run-on sentences. Write one sentence on each line, adding punctuation.

1. my ski club goes to Jack Frost Mountain every Tuesday evening it is so much fun

    _____

    _____

2. I take lessons every year you can never practice too much

    _____

    _____

3. snowboarding looks so cool if you want to learn to snowboard start on easy mountains

    _____

    _____

Underline the subject of each sentence below.

1. The youngest skier on the mountain was three years old.

2. My father cut ski poles to fit me.

3. The yellow ski hat was lost in the snow.

4. People who ski must be careful of the sun.

5. Have you ever skied in the West?

6. These mittens are supposed to be the warmest.

Multiplication Review

Complete the chart with multiplication facts.

X	4	3	7	1	8	10	6	5	2	9
5										
8	32									
10										
4										
7		21								
9										
1										
6										
3										
2										

JOKE CORNER

What does a skunk do when it gets angry?
See page 13 for answer.

What makes an octopus a good fighter?
See page 19 for answer.

What's the best way to talk to a fish?
See page 36 for answer.

Bats

Bats have lived on earth for 50 million years. They live everywhere in the world except the Arctic and Antarctic regions. However, most of the world's bats live in the tropics near the equator because bats prefer warm **climates**.

There are more than 1000 different kinds of bats. The smallest bat has a body about the size of a bumblebee. Can you imagine that! That tiny bat measures five inches from the tip of one wing to the tip of the other. This is called its **wingspan**. The biggest bat has a body about the size of a pigeon and a wingspan of six feet.

Bats come in many different colors. Most bats are brown. However, some bats are black and white. Some even have fur that is red or yellowish in color.

Although bats can fly, they are <u>not</u> related to birds. Bats are **mammals**, like dogs and humans. Like most mammals, they have hair on their bodies and they feed their young with milk. What makes bats so special is that they are the only mammals that can fly like birds. Bats use their hands as wings. Their hands have two layers of strong skin stretched tightly over their long, bony fingers. Bats use their powerful chest and shoulder muscles to move their wings.

Bats are **nocturnal**. This means they are active during the night. They sleep during the day in their homesites called **roosts**. Bats are unusual because they sleep hanging upside down by their toes. When bats are resting, they fold their wings around their bodies for protection.

Bats live in attics, caves, tunnels, trees, and other sheltered places. While some bats live alone, most bats live in **colonies** with other bats. These colonies might only have a dozen or so bats, or they might have millions and millions of bats.

To find their way in the dark of night and to locate food, bats use a kind of sonar called **echolocation**. Like whales in the ocean, bats send out signals from their mouths or nostrils and pick up the returning echoes. These signals are so high they cannot be heard by humans. With their extremely good hearing, bats read these echoes to fly in the dark and to learn what is around them.

For food, bats eat many different kinds of insects including mosquitoes, crickets, winged ants, spiders, moths, and dragonflies. Some bats eat fish, rodents, and other small bats. There is even one type of bat, the vampire bat, that feeds on the blood of cattle and birds. Bats need to eat a lot of food. Some bats eat almost half their weight in insects each night. Their huge appetites for insects make bats very important to our environment.

Write T in front of the statements that are true and F in front of the statements that are false.

_____ 1. Bats have lived on earth for 50 million years.

_____ 2. There are more than 1000 different kinds of bats.

_____ 3. Most bats are brown.

_____ 4. Bats are related to birds.

_____ 5. Bats fly with their hands.

_____ 6. Bats are most active during the day.

Circle the word in each statement that does not belong.

1. A bat's fur can be   black   brown   pink   white   red

2. Bats live in   caves   tunnels   flowers   attics   trees

3. Bats eat   moths   crickets   spiders   vegetables

4. Bats are mammals like   dogs   cats   pigs   birds   horses

5. To fly, a bat uses its   hands   toes   wings   shoulders   chest

Write the plural form of these words.

1. colony _____
2. echo _____
3. color _____

4. muscle _____
5. roost _____
6. body _____

**Write F in front of the statements that are fact and
O in front of the statements that are opinion.**

_____ 1. Bats prefer warm climates to cold climates.

_____ 2. Bats are lazy because they sleep all day.

_____ 3. Bats use echoes to find their food.

_____ 4. Bats are graceful fliers.

_____ 5. Bats eat half their weight in insects.

_____ 6. Bats are ugly.

Draw a line from each word to its correct meaning.

1. mammal   active at night

2. nocturnal   the regular weather in an area

3. colony   locating objects with echoes

4. roost   measurement from tip of one wing to tip of other

5. echolocation   animal that feeds its young with milk

6. climate   a group of animals that live together

7. wingspan   homesite

Indoor Recess

Imagine it's one of those indoor recess days, with your teacher trying to amuse you. Here are some of the questions your teacher uses to test your thinking skills. The faster you can answer them, the sooner you will get to go play on the computer.

1. First, your class wants to buy you a secret birthday gift that costs $45. If the class saved $5 each week, in how many weeks would there be enough money to buy your gift?

   _____

2. Next, your friends have drawn this table on the board. Now they want YOU to fill in the empty squares so that the numbers add up to 15, whether you add up, down, across or even diagonally!

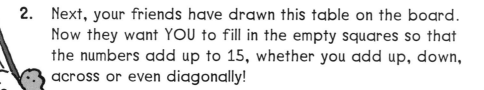

4	3	8
	7	6

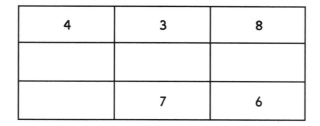

3. Finally, your teacher is going fishing tonight at 6:00. Is that A.M. or P.M.?   _____

4. Then your teacher wants to watch the sunset. Is that A.M. or P.M.?   _____

5. Finally, your teacher wants to take a walk on the beach just as the sun rises. Is that A.M. or P.M.?   _____

Now it's your turn on the computer!

Answer from page 9: It raises a stink.

CRAZY DAY

Complete this story. Use extra paper if you need it.

When I woke up, I was sure that it would just be another lazy, hazy day of summer. I would eat, watch TV, go for a swim, watch TV—you know the summer routine. Was I ever shocked that the lazy, hazy day turned CRAZY! It began as soon as I opened my bedroom door...

_____

_____

_____

_____

_____

_____

_____

_____

_____

_____

_____

_____

_____

_____

_____

_____

_____

Read About It Author Louis Sachar has written many books about Marvin Redpost, including _Marvin Redpost: Why Pick on Me?_ Marvin seems to have crazy days almost all the time!

Round and Round

Round to the nearest ten.

1. 69 = _____

2. 123 = _____

3. 75 = _____

4. 249 = _____

5. 4914 = _____

6. 6789 = _____

Round to the nearest hundred.

1. 340 = _____

2. 625 = _____

3. 109 = _____

4. 190 = _____

5. 2952 = _____

6. 7496 = _____

Round to the nearest thousand.

1. 6666 = _____

2. 3051 = _____

3. 3859 = _____

4. 6720 = _____

5. 1199 = _____

6. 4820 = _____

Spell Check

Circle the word with the correct spelling.

1. Chad swam _____ the pool.
   - accross
   - across
   - accrost
   - acrost

2. Our dog is _____.
   - loset
   - losed
   - lost
   - loss

3. I read the _____.
   - storey
   - storry
   - story
   - stoary

4. _____ is the cat?
   - Were
   - Where
   - Wher
   - Wherr

5. I _____ you went home.
   - thot
   - thaut
   - thoght
   - thought

6. I stayed up _____ dark.
   - until
   - intill
   - untile
   - untill

7. Where have you _____?
   - bin
   - been
   - ben
   - binn

8. I _____ play soccer.
   - mite
   - mit
   - might
   - mitte

9. We _____ eat at noon.
   - usualy
   - usually
   - ussually
   - usaully

10. The room was filled with _____.
    - peeple
    - poeple
    - people
    - poeplle

11. Joe has a big _____.
    - famly
    - familly
    - family
    - famile

12. Kelly knows the _____.
    - anser
    - answer
    - ansser
    - anserr

13. Bess drew a _____.
    - pitcher
    - picter
    - pictur
    - picture

14. Jake rode _____ the tunnel.
    - threw
    - through
    - thruogh
    - threwh

15. They walked _____ the door.
    - tward
    - tored
    - toward
    - towrd

16. Will turned off the _____.
    - lite
    - light
    - litte
    - lit

17. We have _____ food.
    - enuf
    - enough
    - enuff
    - enuogh

18. Jane saw _____ horses.
    - several
    - sevral
    - severel
    - sevreld

16

Fractions

Color the figure to show the fraction. Then write the fraction for the unshaded part on the line. The first one has been done for you.

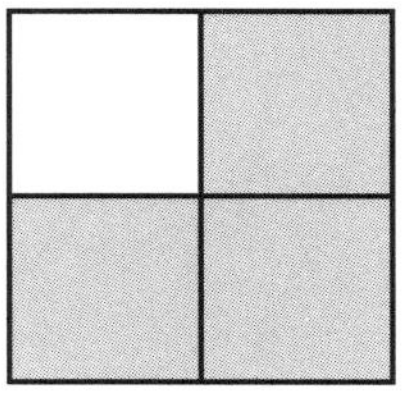

$\frac{3}{4}$ $\frac{1}{4}$

1. 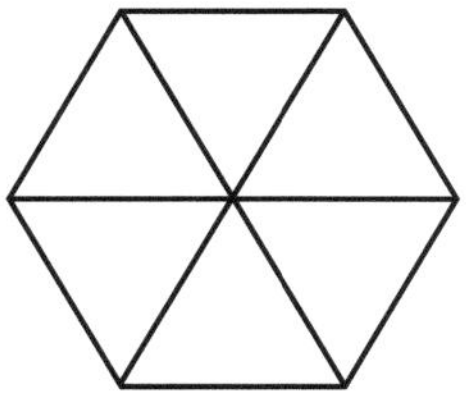

$\frac{2}{6}$ ____

2. 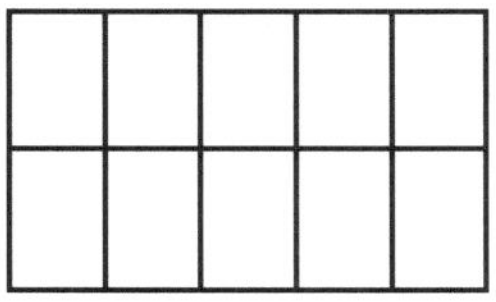

$\frac{4}{10}$ ____

3. 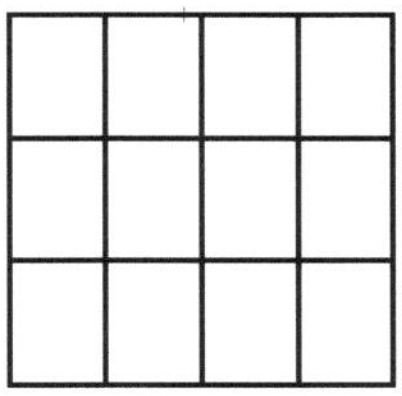

$\frac{5}{12}$ ____

4. 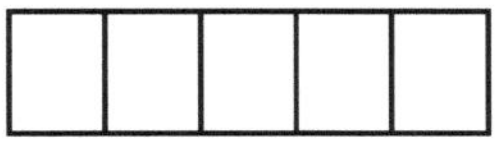

$\frac{1}{5}$ ____

5. 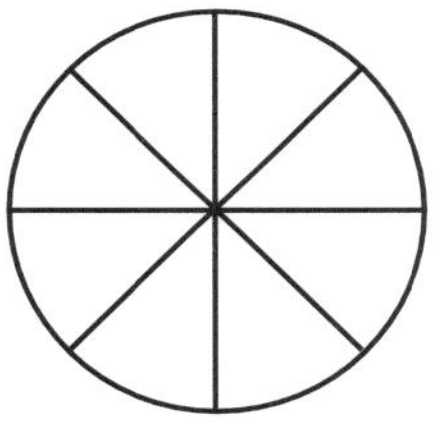

$\frac{3}{8}$ ____

6. 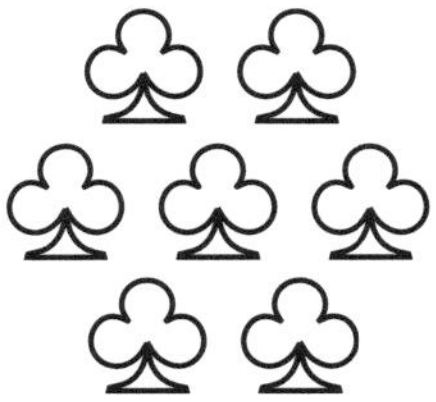

$\frac{3}{7}$ ____

7. 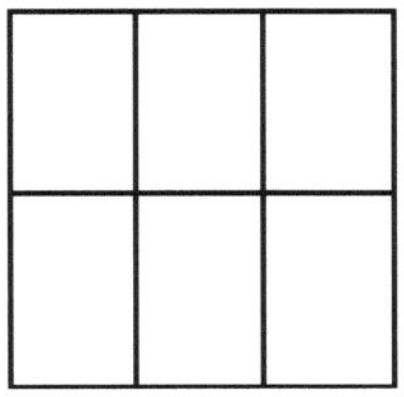

$\frac{1}{6}$ ____

8. 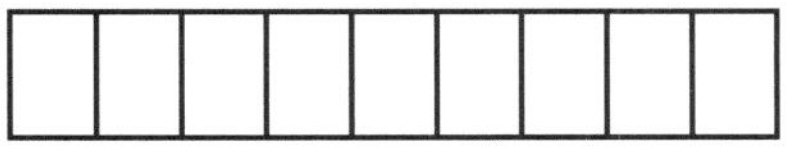

$\frac{4}{9}$ ____

Exploring English

Fill in the circle in front of the group of words that is a sentence.

1. ○ a. The hot summer.
   ● b. The day was hot.
   ○ c. Swam and fished.

2. ○ a. The bait on the line.
   ○ b. Fished for two hours.
   ○ c. The boat was painted red.

3. ○ a. Mike's kite broke.
   ○ b. Tried for hours to get it.
   ○ c. A kite shaped like a fish.

4. ○ a. The swim meet.
   ○ b. I won the freestyle.
   ○ c. Blew the whistle.

Underline the statements. Circle the questions.
Put an X after the commands.

1. We went to the beach in August.

2. Did you go at all this summer?

3. If you went to the beach, raise your hand.

4. Are you sure it was the beach and not the mountains?

5. Be honest!

6. I hope we go to the beach every year.

Underline the subject of the sentences.

1. John went to camp in July.

2. Camp Archbald has been there for twenty years.

3. The sports at the camp were baseball and swimming.

Fill in the circle in front of the sentence in which the predicate is underlined.

1. ○ a. <u>The lifeguards</u> at our pool are skinny.
   ● b. Tom <u>swam to the side</u>.
   ○ c. <u>The trophy</u> was for Lauren.

2. ○ a. My sister <u>loves the baby pool</u>.
   ○ b. <u>I</u> wonder why the baby pool is yellow.
   ○ c. <u>Molly</u> lost her tools in the baby pool.

3. ○ a. <u>The swim meet</u> lasted two hours.
   ○ b. <u>We</u> won the swim meet by 20 points.
   ○ c. Theresa <u>hit the diving board</u>.

Write the base word plus an ending of *s*, *es*, *ed*, or *ing*.

1. How many _____ until we get there?
   mile

2. Why are we _____ instead of flying?
   drive

3. We only brought three _____ with us.
   lunch

4. I made sure all of the _____ were in the car.
   box

5. Mom is _____ all the way to the seashore!
   sleep

6. This road needs to be _____ again!
   pave

Answer from page 9: It is well-armed.

DIZZY NUMBERS

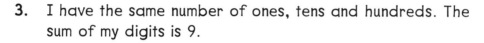

What number am I?

1. I have 6 tens, 8 hundreds and 3 ones.

   What number am I? _____

2. I have 9 ones and 4 hundreds.

   What number am I? _____

3. I have the same number of ones, tens and hundreds. The sum of my digits is 9.

   What number am I? _____

4. I have 4 hundreds. I have 3 more ones than tens. My digits make a sum of 9.

   What number am I? _____

5. The sum of my digits is 12. I have 6 hundreds and 2 ones.

   What number am I? _____

6. The sum of my digits is 14. I have the same number of hundreds and ones. I have 4 tens.

   What number am I? _____

7. I have 4 hundreds, 2 ones, and 3 thousands.

   What number am I? _____

Pandora's Box

More than three thousand years ago, the ancient Greeks used stories called *myths* to make sense of their world. These stories were retold many times and in many different versions. This is one version of the famous story of a young woman named Pandora and a mysterious box.

In ancient times, the Greek gods and goddesses lived high above the clouds on Mount Olympus. The people lived in the valley below. Both the gods and the people were happy. No one had any troubles and there was no pain or sorrow.

This carefree life did not continue forever. One day Zeus, the greatest of the gods, became angry with the people because they did not appreciate all that the gods had given them. To punish them, Zeus had the figure of a beautiful girl molded out of clay. When the figure was finished, Zeus breathed life into her and gave her the name Pandora. Then he called together the other gods and asked them to give her gifts.

Apollo, the god of the arts, taught Pandora to love music. Aphrodite, the goddess of love, gave her beauty. Athene, the goddess of wisdom and the home, taught her to use a spinning wheel. Demeter, the goddess of the harvest, taught her to garden. Poseidon, the god of the sea, gave her a pearl necklace and promised her she would never drown. Zeus gave Pandora a lovely, golden box that was closed tight. He told her that she must **never, never** open this box. Finally, Hera, the jealous queen of the gods, gave Pandora curiosity.

Zeus sent Pandora down to the people in the valley, carrying with her the lovely, golden box that he had given her. Pandora remembered that Zeus told her **never, never** to open the box.

Before long, the beautiful Pandora married a man named Epimetheus. She was so happy as she played music, spun, and tended her garden. But

one thing bothered her: she could not stop wondering what was in the lovely, golden box. She knew she must **never, never** open it, but she so wanted to know what was inside.

To get the box out of her mind, Pandora tried hiding the box in a closet. But the box was always in her thoughts. She tried hiding it in a great wooden chest, but the lovely, golden box would not leave her mind.

One day, when Epimetheus was away, Pandora's curiosity became too great. She had to know what was in the box. She thought, "What harm could come from just taking a peek?" She opened the box a crack and saw nothing. She opened the box a little more. She heard a buzzing sound coming from inside. Unable to control herself any longer, she opened the box all the way.

What an awful mistake! Pandora watched in horror as horrible lizard-like creatures with bat wings flew from the box. They buzzed around the room and then flew out the door. Pandora slammed the lid of the box shut, and as she did, she noticed a bright metal object shining on its bottom. Pandora knew that this object was different from the horrible creatures that had just escaped, but she was too frightened to look. She decided to wait for her husband Epimetheus to come home.

When Epimetheus returned, Pandora told him what had happened. Epimetheus knew what these horrible creatures were. He told Pandora that they were the creatures of unhappiness: Disease, Cruelty, Hatred, War, Pain, and Sorrow. Life would no longer be happy all the time. Once let out, these creatures could never be returned to their box. He told Pandora that Zeus was punishing the people for not thanking the gods enough. But perhaps there was something more. What was the shiny metal object on the bottom of the box?

Together Pandora and Epimetheus lifted the lid of the box. The shiny metal object was no longer there. Instead, out of the box rose a beautiful, fragrant flower. It was a gift from Zeus.

After much thought, Pandora and Epimetheus understood what Zeus was teaching them. He was teaching them to have hope because with **bad,** there is often **good.**

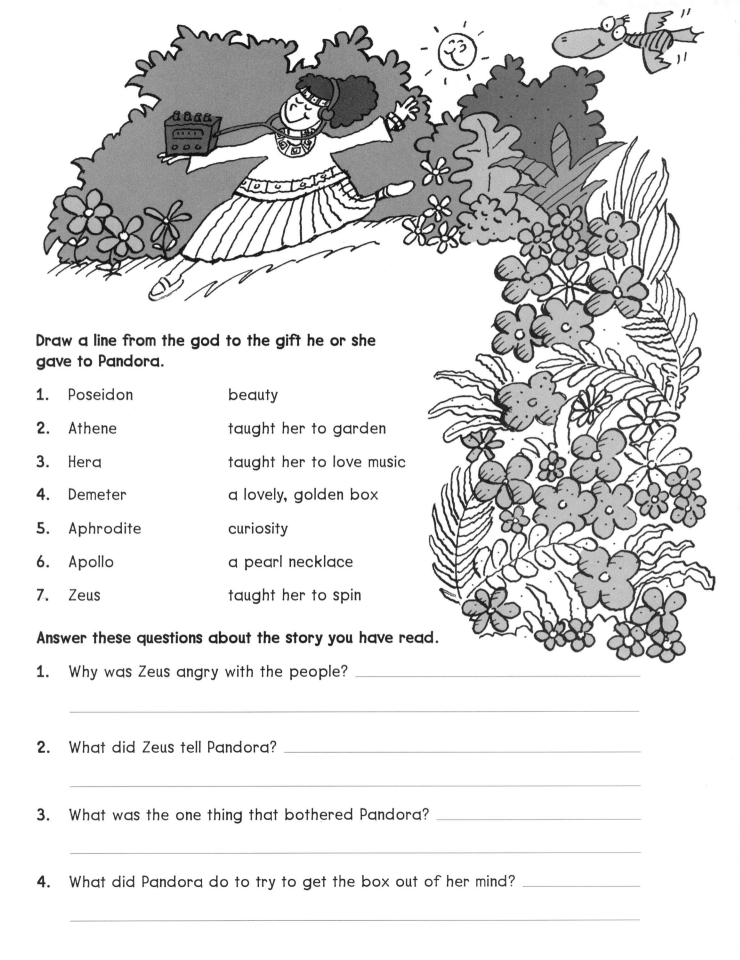

Draw a line from the god to the gift he or she gave to Pandora.

1. Poseidon   beauty

2. Athene   taught her to garden

3. Hera   taught her to love music

4. Demeter   a lovely, golden box

5. Aphrodite   curiosity

6. Apollo   a pearl necklace

7. Zeus   taught her to spin

Answer these questions about the story you have read.

1. Why was Zeus angry with the people? _____

_____

2. What did Zeus tell Pandora? _____

_____

3. What was the one thing that bothered Pandora? _____

_____

4. What did Pandora do to try to get the box out of her mind? _____

_____

5. What were the horrible creatures that escaped from the box?

_____

_____

_____

6. What rose out of the box when Pandora and Epimetheus
lifted its lid? _____

_____

_____

7. You may have heard someone warn a friend, "I wouldn't do
that. You may be opening a Pandora's box." What do you
think that person means?

_____

_____

_____

_____

Circle the answer to each question.

1. Zeus called the clay figure of the girl _____.

   Hera   Epimetheus   Pandora

2. You can decide from reading the story that _____.
   Pandora liked pearl necklaces.
   Pandora was very curious.
   Pandora was an evil person.

3. What did Pandora notice on the bottom of the box?
   a horrible monster
   a key
   a shiny metal object

4. What was Zeus teaching Pandora and Epimetheus?
   People should love each other.
   With bad, there is often good.
   Flowers are very beautiful.

Many famous artists have painted pictures of Greek myths. Pretend that you are a famous artist who has been asked to paint a picture of Pandora opening the lovely, golden box. Instead of oil paints, you will use colored pencils or crayons.

Wagon Wheels

Fill in the missing numbers (addends) on the wheels.

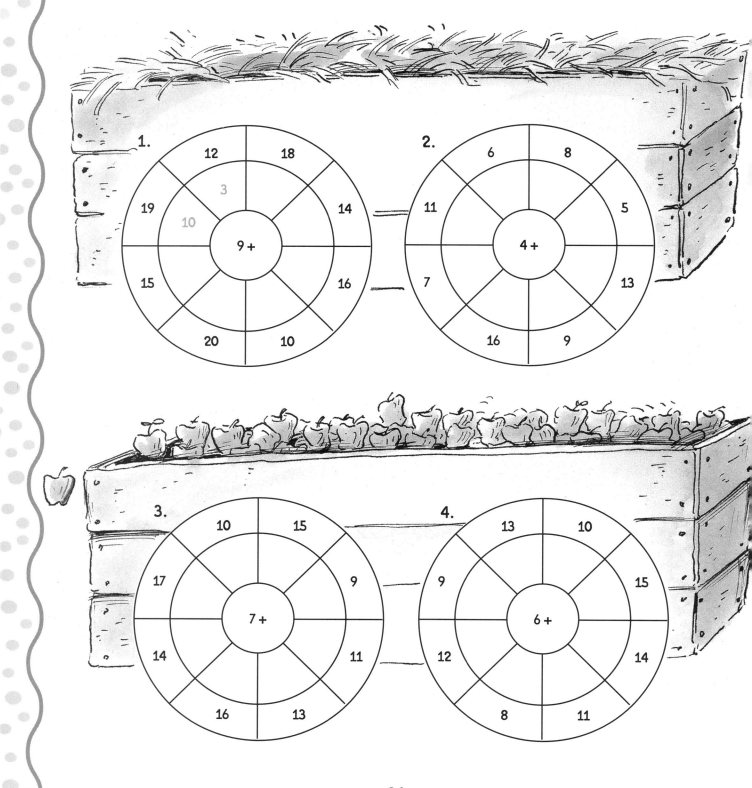

1. 9 +
  - 12, 18, 3, 10, 14, 16, 10, 20, 15, 19

2. 4 +
  - 6, 8, 5, 13, 9, 16, 7, 11

3. 7 +
  - 10, 15, 9, 11, 13, 16, 14, 17

4. 6 +
  - 13, 10, 15, 14, 11, 8, 12, 9

Lemonade for Sale

During the first week in August, Emily and Matt had a lemonade sale. The table below shows the number of glasses of lemonade they sold on each date.

Use the information in the table to complete the line graph. Then answer the questions using the line graph you have made.

Date	Glasses Sold
August 1	10
August 2	25
August 3	15
August 4	30
August 5	35
August 6	20
August 7	25

1. On what date did they sell the most glasses of lemonade?

   _____

2. On what dates did they sell the same number of glasses?

   _____

3. On what dates did they sell fewer than twenty-five glasses?

   _____

4. If each glass of lemonade cost 10¢, how much money did they make on August 3? _____

   On August 1? _____

5. What was the total number of glasses sold? _____

6. How much money did they collect during the whole week?

Mishmash

Questions	Answers

1. Name 2 words that begin with "kn" (example: knee).

2. A map is a flat drawing of the earth. What do you call a map on a sphere or ball?

3. How many years in a century?

4. Which is not a state: Pennsylvania, New Jersey, Philadelphia, Ohio

5. How many continents on earth?

6. Which is farther south: Florida or New York?

7. Which is closer to an ocean: Colorado or Maine?

8. What are the vowels?

9. If a letter is not a vowel, what is it called?

10. You walked for $1\frac{1}{2}$ hours. How many minutes did you walk?

11. What word means the same as 12 o'clock at night?

12. Is the sun a planet or a star?

13. How many minutes in an hour?

14. How many hours in a day?

15. What makes sound: vibration or friction?

16. What makes heat: vibration or friction?

Questions	Answers

17. Who is the president of the United States now?

18. How many angles does a triangle have?

19. Spell the second month of the year.

20. Who was the first president of the United States?

21. What is the home of a honeybee called?

22. What animal has a pouch for its young children?

23. Things are either solid, liquid, or what?

24. Which is larger: $\frac{1}{2}$ or $\frac{1}{3}$ of something?

25. What do we call a mass of ice in the ocean?

26. How many sides does a pentagon have?

27. Finish the pattern: 25, 50, 75, _____

28. What uses gills to breathe?

29. How many months in $1\frac{1}{2}$ years?

30. What kind of energy runs your television and computer?

31. What planet is most known for the rings around it?

32. How many cups in a pint?

What Did You Say?

The English language has many colorful sayings. Some of these sayings are underlined in the left hand column. Match the 7 sayings in the left column to their correct meanings in the right column by writing your answer on the line. The first one has been done for you.

<u>7</u>   Are you still mad at me for breaking your bike? <u>Don't cry over spilled milk!</u>

_____   Be careful, Sue. <u>You are going from the frying pan to the fire!</u>

_____   Stop looking out the window. <u>A watched pot never boils.</u>

_____   John, this picture for your report is not good. <u>Back to the drawing board!</u>

_____   I thought that you were going to ask Sally for a date. <u>Are you getting cold feet?</u>

_____   Invite that new boy over. <u>Don't judge a book by its cover.</u>

_____   I want to know exactly how you did on that science quiz. <u>Don't beat around the bush!</u>

1.   Start over from the beginning.

2.   Don't try to avoid answering the question.

3.   You are going from one dangerous situation to another.

4.   You are nervous or scared about something.

5.   If you wait for something without doing anything else, it will seem to take forever.

6.   You can't tell what someone or something is really like just by looking at its appearance.

7.   Once something is done or lost, don't waste time worrying about it.

 **Read About It** Fred Gwynne uses language in a fun way (as you can tell from the title) in his book *A Chocolate Moose for Dinner*.

Challenge

Round to the nearest ten, hundred, and thousand.

	10's	100's	1000's
1434			
6727			
984			
2952			
3051			
6666			

1. $36 \div 9 =$ **2.** $42 \div 7 =$ **3.** $45 \div 9 =$

4. $56 \div 7 =$ **5.** $24 \div 4 =$ **6.** $81 \div 9 =$

7. $9 \div 1 =$ **8.** $20 \div 0 =$ **9.** $49 \div 7 =$

10. $45 \div 5 =$ **11.** $24 \div 3 =$ **12.** $64 \div 8 =$

13. $7 \div 1 =$ **14.** $14 \div 2 =$ **15.** $36 \div 6 =$

16. $30 \div 3 =$ **17.** $72 \div 8 =$ **18.** $21 \div 7 =$

19. $54 \div 6 =$ **20.** $63 \div 9 =$ **21.** $77 \div 7 =$

Ship's Wheels

Multiply to fill in the outside of each circle.

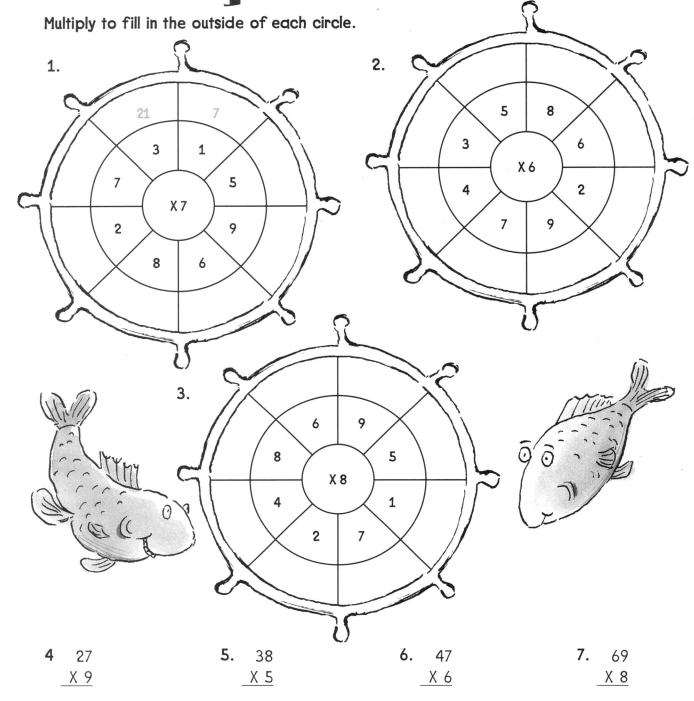

1.

(X 7) 3, 1, 5, 9, 6, 8, 2, 7   21   7

2.

(X 6) 5, 8, 6, 2, 9, 7, 4, 3

3.

(X 8) 6, 9, 5, 1, 7, 2, 4, 8

4	27 X 9	5.	38 X 5	6.	47 X 6	7.	69 X 8
8.	73 X 4	9.	86 X 7	10.	54 X 3	11.	94 X 9

Book Club

You and your friends have signed up for the library's summer reading program. Each time you go to the library, you tell the librarian how many books you have read. At the end of the summer, the librarian records the number of books on a bar graph.

NAME

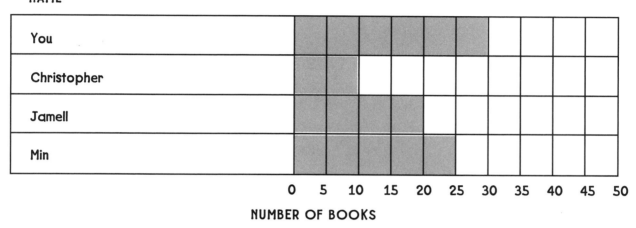

NUMBER OF BOOKS

Use the bar graph to answer these questions.

1. How many books did you read this summer? _____

2. Who read the most books this summer? _____

3. How many more books did Jamell read than Christopher? _____

4. Which two friends together read the same number of books as you?

    _____   _____

5. How many books did you and Min read together? _____

6. What is the total number of books you and your friends read this summer?

    _____

At the Movies

Homonyms: Words that sound the same but have different meanings

Choose the correct homonym for each sentence.

1. We _____ our bicycles to the movie theater.
   road rode

2. Although he was scared, Jason watched the _____ movie.
   hole whole

3. "Who _____ how this movie will end?" Ted asked.
   knows nose

4. Julie had enough money to _____ popcorn and a soda.
   by buy

5. As the _____ set in the west, the cowboys rode into town.
   sun son

6. "My grandpa's favorite movie is *1001 Arabian* _____," said Rob.
   Nights Knights

JOKE CORNER

What do you call a group of large actors?
See page 59 for answer.

Cineplex

The Cineplex has four theaters showing movies at the same time.
These four clocks show what time each movie starts. Write the
time below each clock.

Theater 1   Theater 2   Theater 3   Theater 4

_____   _____   _____   _____

These four clocks show what time each movie ends.
Write the time below each clock.

Theater 1   Theater 2   Theater 3   Theater 4

_____   _____   _____   _____

Use both sets of clocks to tell the length of each movie.

Theater 1   Theater 2   Theater 3   Theater 4

____ _____   ____ _____   ____ _____   ____ _____
hours minutes   hours minutes   hours minutes   hours minutes

How Much Does It Hold?

Circle the better unit of measurement.

1. The water in a swimming pool   cup   gallon

2. A glass of soda   quart   cup

3. A pitcher of lemonade   cup   quart

```
KEY
2 CUPS    =    1 PINT
2 PINTS   =    1 QUART
4 CUPS    =    1 QUART
4 QUARTS  =    1 GALLON
```

Use the key to help you answer these questions.

1. How many cups are in 2 quarts? _____

2. How many quarts are in 3 gallons? _____

3. How many cups are in 2 pints? _____

4. How many quarts are in 4 gallons? _____

5. How many cups are in 1 gallon? _____

6. Sandy is making lemonade to sell. She needs 4 cups of water for each can of lemonade mix. She wants to use 3 cans of lemonade mix. How many cups of water will she need? _____ How many quarts is this? _____

7. Will is having a party. Including Will, there will be 8 people at the party. He wants to buy quarts of soda. He figures each person will drink 2 cups of soda. How many cups of soda does he figure he will need? _____

   How many quarts of soda does he need to buy? _____

Answer from page 9: Drop it a line.

36

Hubble Who?

A telescope is an instrument that makes a distant object bigger so that we can see it better. Telescopes gather light from the distant object and focus it, increasing the intensity of the light and allowing the object to be magnified or enlarged. Most modern telescopes use mirrors to collect light.

In 1609, Galileo invented the telescope. Ever since that time, scientists have been trying to improve upon his invention. One American who worked with telescopes in the early 1900s and who made many important discoveries was Edwin Hubble.

Scientists using telescopes on Earth must look up through the atmosphere of Earth in order to study stars and other planets. No matter how large the telescope (and some are huge!), the atmosphere causes a blur and scientists cannot see clearly what is being studied.

On April 24, 1990, a dream came true for many scientists. The space shuttle *Discovery* dropped into space a huge telescope called the Hubble Space Telescope. No longer would scientists have to study distant objects through Earth's atmosphere. The pictures sent back by the Hubble would be free from the blur caused by Earth's atmosphere. The Hubble Space Telescope would allow scientists to peer into the farthest and oldest corners of our universe.

The Hubble Space Telescope, named after Edwin Hubble, cost $1.6 billion dollars. Therefore, it is not surprising that when the telescope began to have problems within two months after it was put into space, many Americans were disappointed. Some were even angry that so much money was "wasted."

Perhaps the Hubble's biggest problem was with the mirror that collected light. The mirror needed to have a precise curve so that the telescope could focus. However, one edge was too flat—by an amount that one cannot even see with the naked eye! That meant that the telescope sent fuzzy images back to Earth.

A second major problem was caused by the huge changes in temperature that occur in space. The wing-like objects on the telescope that collected energy from the sun were expanding (getting bigger) because of the heat during the day and contracting (getting smaller) because of the cold during the night. This caused the telescope to "shiver." Scientists were afraid that this shivering would hurt the telescope's delicate instruments.

A third problem had to do with the gyroscopes. Gyroscopes are instruments that look like a child's top. They spin and help steady the telescope. Three of the six gyroscopes on the Hubble had already broken. If any more broke, the telescope could not be accurately pointed in the direction of the object it was studying.

Because of the cost of repair, people argued whether the telescope could or should be fixed. Scientists finally decided to go ahead and fix the Hubble.

After incredible preparation and training, astronauts flew the space shuttle *Endeavor* from the Kennedy Space Center in Cape Canaveral, Florida, into space. It took the *Endeavor* two days to catch up to the Hubble. The astronauts on the *Endeavor* had only ONE chance to catch the Hubble with the robot arm of the shuttle. If they missed grabbing the Hubble, there would not be enough fuel for a second try.

Because of their intense preparation, the astronauts on board the *Endeavor* were able to catch the Hubble on their first try. Over the next few days they took turns going outside the *Endeavor* to repair the Hubble. Much of what they had to do was dangerous and scary. Things that may seem unimportant, like dropping a screw, could turn into a disaster in space. In fact, a tiny screw did come loose and floated away as the astronauts were outside the *Endeavor* making repairs on the Hubble. The problem was serious because in space, where there is no gravity, a tiny floating screw could crash into and damage the Hubble. Therefore, one of the astronauts had to ride the mechanical arm of the *Endeavor* while another astronaut inside the *Endeavor* steered him toward the floating screw. The screw was retrieved.

The scientists shared joy and relief when the Hubble was repaired. The astronauts returned safely to Earth. Because of their skill and bravery, the world now had the extraordinary Hubble Space Telescope to see far beyond where humans had ever seen before.

Read About It *Adventure in Space—The Flight to Fix the Hubble*, by Elaine Scott and Margaret Miller, is a thorough and amazing account of the Hubble mission.

Did you get the facts?

1. What do telescopes use to collect light? _____

2. How is the Hubble telescope different from other telescopes?

   _____

   _____

   _____

3. What space shuttle took the Hubble into space?

   _____

4. What space shuttle took the astronauts into space to fix the Hubble?

   _____

Write T in front of the statements that are true and F in front of the statements that are false.

_____ 1. The Hubble Space Telescope was made by Edwin Hubble.

_____ 2. Edwin Hubble lived in Russia and studied telescopes.

_____ 3. The Hubble Space Telescope worked for almost a decade before it broke.

_____ 4. The Hubble Space Telescope cost $1.6 billion dollars.

_____ 5. The *Endeavor* astronauts only had one chance to grab the telescope from space.

_____ 6. The Hubble Space Telescope was so faraway that it took the *Endeavor* three weeks to catch it in space.

Write F if the statement is a fact. Write O if the statement is an opinion.

_____ 1. The Hubble has six gyroscopes to help steady it.

_____ 2. Scientists who study telescopes are the most important scientists.

_____ 3. It is wise to spend so much money exploring space.

_____ 4. Heat causes materials to expand (get larger). Cold causes materials to contract (get smaller.)

Write the letter of the definition in front of the word.

_____ telescope   **a.**   exact

_____ invention   **b.**   picture or likeness

_____ blur   **c.**   an instrument that enlarges a distant object

_____ precise   **d.**   extreme

_____ image   **e.**   a device that someone makes for the first time

_____ intense   **f.**   smear

BLAST OFF!

Your school has been asked to supply a few students to travel on the next space mission. YOU have been chosen to go, along with three of your friends. The four of you will travel with two real astronauts to a space station and stay there for one week before returning home.

Write about your adventure. Use extra paper as needed.

_____

_____

_____

_____

_____

_____

_____

_____

_____

_____

_____

_____

_____

_____

_____

_____

_____

_____

_____

Calendars

You will need a calendar to answer these questions.

1. How many days are there in a week? _____

2. Which months have 30 days? _____

   _____

3. Which months have 31 days? _____

   _____

4. Which month has fewer than 30 days? _____

   How many days does it have? _____

5. Using the information you have gathered in questions 2, 3, and 4, how many

   days are there in this year? _____

6. What day is 4 days later than Sunday? _____

7. Write the day or the month.

   Feb. _____   Tues. _____

   Fri. _____   Oct. _____

   Sun. _____   Aug. _____

8. Write the abbreviation.

   January _____

   Saturday _____

   Monday _____

   September _____

   Wednesday _____

   December _____

Tiger Tough Math

Fill in the missing numbers.

1.
```
  6 8 9 7
- 3 _ 5 1
---------
  3 4 4 _
```

2.
```
  9 7 5 3
- _ 5 1 _
---------
  4 2 3 9
```

3.
```
  2 _ 0 3
- 1 9 8 1
---------
  0 0 2 _
```

4.
```
  _ 7 _
- 3 4 6
-------
  0 2 6
```

5.
```
  6 _ 5 7
-   3 2 9
---------
  _ 5 2 _
```

6.
```
  _ 0 7 5
- 4 8 8 1
---------
  4 1 _ 4
```

7.
```
  359
X   6
-----
```

8.
```
  572
X   8
-----
```

9.
```
  890
X   4
-----
```

10.
```
   57
X   6
-----
```

BONUS: Adventure Safari takes people into the jungle to look at wild animals. Each safari takes 134 people. There are 7 safaris going into the jungle each day. How many people can go on safaris each day? _____

45

Lady Liberty

People throughout the world **recognize** the picture on this page. It is a picture of the Statue of Liberty, the tallest **statue** in the world. For over 100 years, the Statue of Liberty has stood on an island in New York harbor. Lady Liberty, as the Statue of Liberty is often called, welcomes people who come from other countries to live in America. These people, called **immigrants**, see Lady Liberty as a **symbol** of freedom and opportunity.

The Statue of Liberty was built by a Frenchman, Frédéric Auguste Bartholdi. He, along with other Frenchmen, wanted to give a gift to the United States to show the long friendship between the two countries and to recognize the ideal of **liberty** shared by both countries.

In 1871, Mr. Bartholdi sailed from France to America to gain support for the statue. He landed in New York **harbor**. He looked around and decided that it was the perfect place for his statue because New York harbor was "where people get their first view of the new world."

It was agreed that France would pay for the statue and America would pay for the statue's base, or **pedestal**. Huge **fundraising** events were held in both France and America to raise the money needed for the project.

Mr. Bartholdi's plans called for a 305-foot-tall statue constructed from a huge skeleton of iron and steel, covered with a thin layer of copper. The statue would be of a proud woman dressed in a flowing robe. At her feet, there would be a ***broken chain*** showing that the United States had broken free from Great Britain. In her left hand, Liberty would hold a ***tablet***.

On the tablet would be written July 4, 1776, the date of America's independence. In her right hand, she would hold a burning ***torch*** to welcome people to America. On her head, she would wear a ***crown*** with 7 rays standing for the hope that the American ideals of liberty would be spread across the 7 seas to the 7 continents.

Construction of the statue was begun in Paris, France, in 1875. Mr. Bartholdi wanted to finish the statue's arm and torch in time for America's celebration of its first 100 years, called the **centennial** celebration. Three hundred thousand Frenchmen paid to watch Bartholdi and his men build his statue! Twenty men worked 10 hours a day, 7 days a week.

At last, the 30-foot-tall arm and torch section of Lady Liberty was completed and shipped to America before the end of the centennial celebration. It was displayed in Philadelphia, where the Centennial Exhibition was being held. Visitors paid 50¢ to climb a ladder to the balcony surrounding the torch. People became very excited about the first statue you could climb inside.

Mr. Bartholdi's next goal was to build the 17-foot-high head of Lady Liberty in time for the opening of the Paris World's Fair two years later. But raising money for this incredibly expensive statue was very hard. The copper head of Lady Liberty got to the World's Fair in 1878, but a little late. Once it arrived, however, it was a sensation. People loved that the head was huge! The nose was almost 5 feet long and the mouth was 3 feet wide!

Lady Liberty was finished in 1884, almost 9 years after she was started. She was displayed in Paris, France, until 1885, when the job of bringing the statue to America was begun. To get the Statue of Liberty from France to America, the statue was taken apart and packed into 214 **crates**. It took almost a year to put her back together piece by piece at her new home in New York harbor.

The Statue of Liberty was finally unveiled to the American public on October 28, 1886, 11 years after the statue was begun. The day was declared a public holiday in America. More than one million people came to watch the parade in New York. The president of the United States, President Grover Cleveland, was there. New York harbor was full of boats. Mr. Bartholdi stood alone in the head of the statue. He pulled the cord that dropped a veil covering the statue's face. The whole world cheered for Lady Liberty.

From the 1890s to the 1920s, millions of immigrants passed the Statue of Liberty as they entered the United States through New York harbor. It was often the first sight immigrants saw of their new country, symbolizing the freedom and opportunities that awaited them in their new homeland.

Today, visitors from all over the world come to see the Statue of Liberty. Visitors can take an elevator to the foot of the statue, where they can go out onto an observation deck. If they are strong climbers, they can climb 354 steps to an observation deck in the crown. From the crown, visitors have a superb view of New York harbor. It is a worthwhile trip for all to visit this magnificent symbol of freedom and opportunity.

1. What name is the Statue of Liberty often called?

   _____

2. Who was in charge of building the statue?

   _____

3. What country gave the Statue of Liberty to America?

   _____

4. What did France and America have in common? (circle one)

   the same president

   the love of liberty

   the same birthday

5. Why did Mr. Bartholdi choose New York harbor as the home for Lady Liberty? _____

6. What part of Lady Liberty did France pay for?

   _____

7. What part of Lady Liberty did America pay for?

   _____

8. What was displayed in Philadelphia in 1876?

   _____

9. What was displayed in Paris in 1878? _____

10. On what date was the statue unveiled in America? _____

11. How long did it take from the beginning of the statue's construction in Paris until it was unveiled in New York?

    _____

Draw a line from the part of the Statue of Liberty to what it represents.

1. torch   freedom from England

2. tablet   liberty spreading across 7 seas

3. crown with 7 rays   Independence Day

4. broken chain   light to welcome people to America

49

Write the number of the correct meaning in the blank next to each word.

_____ recognize	**1.**	freedom
_____ statue	**2.**	an object that stands for something
_____ immigrant	**3.**	identify
_____ symbol	**4.**	box for shipping
_____ liberty	**5.**	a place of shelter for ships
_____ pedestal	**6.**	100 years
_____ centennial	**7.**	figure of a person or animal
_____ crate	**8.**	base supporting a statue
_____ harbor	**9.**	collecting money for a project or group
_____ fundraising	**10.**	someone who comes to a new country

Write F before the statements that are fact and O before the statements that are opinion.

_____ **1.** The Statue of Liberty is the world's tallest statue.

_____ **2.** Mr. Bartholdi was a very clever man.

_____ **3.** The Statue of Liberty is a symbol of freedom.

_____ **4.** The Statue of Liberty is the world's prettiest statue.

_____ **5.** The Statue of Liberty was shipped in 214 crates.

_____ **6.** America paid for the statue's pedestal.

Your Most Unforgettable Moment

Draw a picture of the most unforgettable thing that happened this summer or the most unforgettable thing that ever happened to you.

Nouns Galore

A noun is a person, a place, or a thing.

In each sentence, circle the one underlined word that is a noun.

1. Jenny liked the beautiful flowers.

2. Jaime rode his bike fast.

3. That man climbed a big rock.

4. The children walked the big dog.

In each sentence, circle the one underlined noun that is singular (showing one thing).

1. The pots and pans are in the sink.

2. The boy carried the bats and balls.

3. Their mother locked the doors and windows.

4. The bird ate nuts and berries.

In each sentence, circle the one underlined noun that is plural (showing more than one thing).

1. The boys sent a picture to their uncle.

2. The children visited their grandmother and grandfather.

3. The people swept the driveway and the sidewalk.

4. The dogs chased the cat and the rabbit.

Circle the noun that should be used in each sentence to show ownership.

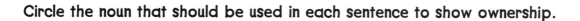

1. My _____ name is Marie.
   aunt aunt's aunts'

2. His _____ names are
   uncle uncle's uncles'
   Joe and Peter.

3. The _____ uniforms
   player player's players'
   were dirty.

4. The _____ books
   children children's childrens'
   got wet.

Most *nouns* are common *nouns*.
They start with **lowercase letters**.

Circle the one underlined noun that is a common noun.

1. Austin is the capital of Texas.

2. My dogs' names are Max and Jill.

3. Paris is a city in France.

4. Thanksgiving and Valentine's Day are my favorite holidays.

A proper *noun* is a particular person, place,
or thing. **It starts with a capital letter.**

Circle the one underlined noun that is a proper noun.

1. My school starts the day after Labor Day.

2. Her friends had a party for Emily.

3. We are taking a trip to England.

4. The boys rode a raft on the Colorado River.

Cross out the one plural noun in each line that is *not* spelled correctly.

1. countries	berries	ladys	fairies	babies
2. classes	ranches	matches	boxes	watchs
3. halves	hooves	lives	leaves	wifes
4. toys	donkeys	valleyes	monkeys	boys

Shadow Experiment

Try this experiment.

1. Go into a dark room. Hold your hand about 1 foot from a wall. Shine a flashlight on your hand. The light goes around your hand and between your fingers. But, it does not go through your hand! A shadow is formed on the wall when your hand blocks out the light. A shadow gives us the outline of an object but shows no other details.

2. Shortly after breakfast on a sunny morning, get a piece of chalk and go outside with a friend to a flat area like your driveway or sidewalk.

   a. Stand with your back to the sun. Have your friend draw your footprints. Then, have your friend trace your shadow.

   b. Using a tape measure, measure the length of your shadow. Record the information in the chart below.

   c. Next, note the direction your shadow is pointing. Record the information.

3. At midday and then late in the afternoon stand in those same footprints. Record the length and direction of your shadow below.

Time of day	Length of shadow How many feet? / How many inches?	Direction of shadow

4. At what time was your shadow the longest? _____

5. At midday, was your shadow long or short? _____

6. Where did it point at the end of the day? _____

7. What can you conclude from the data you have recorded?

_____

_____

Your teacher asked you to help get ready for the school fair by answering these questions.

1. It takes 2¹/₂ hours for your friend, Emily, to drive from Grandmother's house to your school. The fair starts at 7:00 P.M. By what time must Emily leave to arrive at the fair when it starts?

   _____

2. If there are 436 students in the school, and 213 bought tickets in advance, how many did not purchase tickets in advance?

   _____

3. This year the fair committee spent $11,394.00 getting ready for the fair. Last year they spent $6,789.00. How much more did they spend this year than last?

   _____

4. Your principal stepped on the scale and weighed 196 pounds. Then your principal stepped on the scale holding a jar of jelly beans and weighed 214 pounds. How many pounds did the jar of jelly beans weigh?

   _____

Read About It Is math as bad as it seems? Find out in *Math Curse* by Jon Scieszka.

All the News

The stories in newspapers and magazines are called <u>articles</u>.
Find an interesting article in a newspaper or magazine.
Read the article; then answer the following questions.

1. **What** is the title of your article? _____

    _____

2. **What** is the main idea of your article? _____

    _____

    _____

3. **Where** does the event described in your article take place? _____

    _____

4. **When** does the event described in your article take place? _____

    _____

5. **Why** do you think your newspaper article is important? _____

    _____

    _____

A noun is a person, place, or thing. Fill in the chart below
with nouns from your article.

Person nouns	Place nouns	Thing nouns

Eating Out

$1.25 (hot dog)

$2.80 (hamburger)

$.65 (soda)

$2.43 (soup)

$.91 (fries)

$2.00 (sundae)

Answer the questions using the above prices. Show your work.

1. Ken, Sarah, Will, and Kimberly are eating out at Buster's Burgers and Fries. Ken orders a hot dog, french fries, and a soda. How much money does his meal cost? _____

   He has a five dollar bill. How much change does he get? _____

2. Sarah would like a hamburger, a soda, and a bowl of soup. She counts her money and finds that she has four one dollar bills. Does she have enough money? _____

   If not, how much more money does she need? _____

3. Will is very hungry. He orders a hamburger, two orders of french fries, and a soda. How much money does his meal cost? _____

4. Kimberly's mother gave her a ten dollar bill to buy ice cream sundaes for the four of them. If Kimberly buys a hot dog and a soda, will she have enough money left for the sundaes? _____

NUMBER NUTS

Solve these multiplication and division problems.

1. $0.09
   X   6

2. $1.93
   X   8

3. $2.74
   X   7

4. $8.72
   X   8

5. $9.65
   X   6

6. $3.46
   X   5

Hint: There are no remainders!

7. 3844 ÷ 4 =

8. 3367 ÷ 7 =

9. 2304 ÷ 9 =

Hint: These have remainders!

10. 2635 ÷ 8 =

11. 2999 ÷ 3 =

12. 3080 ÷ 6 =

Solve these word problems.

1. Kristin put 8 pieces of chocolate candy in each box.
   She had 72 pieces of candy.

   How many boxes did she fill? _____

2. Lauren can read 6 pages a minute.

   How many pages can she read in 7 minutes? _____

3. Each box of nails costs $4. Each box of screws costs $9 each. How much would 3 boxes of each cost?

_____

4. Each rosebush has 8 flowers. If there are a total of 64 flowers, how many bushes are there?

_____

5. Kelly has three friends in each class. If she has 6 classes, how many friends does she have?

_____

6. Mom bought 6 packages of cupcakes. Each package had 4 cupcakes. Three cupcakes were left. How many were eaten?

_____

These might trick you!

1. 180 X _____ = 180

2. 1763 X _____ = 0

3. 31 + 31 + 31 + 31 = 31 X _____

4. 27 + 27 + 27 + 27 + 27 = 5 X _____

5. 7 X 9 = 9 X _____

6. _____ ÷ 11 = 0

7. _____ ÷ 1 = 654

8. 9 X _____ = 72

Write the related math sentences for 8 X 6 = 48.

_____ X _____ = _____

_____ ÷ _____ = _____

_____ ÷ _____ = _____

Answer from page 34: A broad cast.

59

Capitals and More

Circle all the letters that should be capitals.

In each ☐ , write . or ? or ! to complete the sentence.

1. michael lives at 23 poplar street ☐

2. did amy visit the parkland zoo ☐

3. ted has visited both the atlantic ocean and the pacific ocean ☐

4. my grandmother and aunt barbara live in carson city, kansas ☐

5. lauren goes to fourth street elementary school ☐

6. have you ever visited new york city ☐

Fill in the blank with *to, too,* or *two.*

1. Taisha and Amika went _____ the movies.

2. The children saw _____ horses in the field.

3. I like _____ play soccer and

   Billy does, _____ .

4. She was _____ tired _____ stay up late.

5. Robby bought _____ loaves

   of bread _____ give _____ his mother.

Fraction Frolic

Add or subtract these fractions.

1. $\frac{4}{8} + \frac{2}{8} =$

2. $\frac{6}{12} - \frac{3}{12} =$

3. $\frac{30}{55} - \frac{10}{55} =$

4. $\frac{14}{100} + \frac{3}{100} =$

Change to a mixed number.

1. $\frac{10}{3} = 3\frac{1}{3}$ 2. $\frac{22}{7} =$ 3. $\frac{9}{2} =$ 4. $\frac{5}{4} =$

5. $\frac{26}{24} =$ 6. $\frac{72}{10} =$ 7. $\frac{8}{3} =$ 8. $\frac{7}{6} =$

Change to an improper fraction.

1. $1\frac{3}{4} = \frac{7}{4}$ 2. $5\frac{3}{10} =$ 3. $6\frac{4}{7} =$ 4. $8\frac{2}{9} =$

5. $2\frac{3}{9} =$ 6. $8\frac{2}{7} =$ 7. $7\frac{5}{6} =$ 8. $2\frac{2}{5} =$

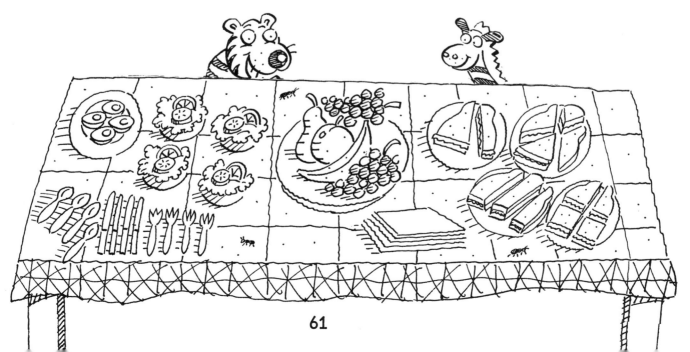

Put these fractions in order from least to greatest.

1. $\frac{6}{20}$ $\frac{4}{5}$ $\frac{1}{2}$ _____

2. $\frac{7}{8}$ $\frac{1}{4}$ $\frac{3}{4}$ $\frac{1}{2}$ _____

3. $\frac{2}{18}$ $\frac{1}{6}$ $\frac{2}{3}$ $\frac{4}{9}$ _____

Solve.

1. The ride to camp took 81 minutes. Andrew slept three-ninths of the time. How long did he sleep? _____

2. Catherine caught 28 fish. Two-sevenths of the fish were brown. How many fish were brown? _____

3. $523 \times 64 =$ _____

4. $66 \times 51 =$ _____

5. $406 \times 36 =$ _____

Cleopatra

Cleopatra is often called the Queen of the Nile because she ruled Egypt, which is located along the Nile River.

Although Cleopatra lived long ago (she was born in 69 B.C.), the Great Pyramids of Egypt had already been standing for more than 2500 years when she was born!

Cleopatra was married to her ten-year-old brother, Ptolemy XIII. This was the custom of some ancient civilizations. At age ten Ptolemy became King of Egypt, and eighteen-year-old Cleopatra became the Queen of Egypt.

Since Ptolemy was just ten years old, some older men, called his advisors, made all of his decisions. The advisors did not like Cleopatra. When Cleopatra was twenty years old, she found out that her brother's advisors were planning to kill her. She ran from Egypt and hid to save her life.

Julius Caesar, the ruler of the Roman Empire, went to Egypt and tried to make peace between Ptolemy's advisors and Cleopatra. He arranged a meeting between them. However, because Ptolemy's advisors were trying to kill Cleopatra, she had to sneak into Egypt. Legend says that she came to the palace meeting hiding in a rolled-up rug! At this meeting, Cleopatra and Julius Caesar fell in love. They lived as husband and wife.

Julius Caesar and Cleopatra fought a war with Ptolemy to win control of Egypt. The war lasted six months. Ptolemy's army lost. Ptolemy, now fifteen years old, drowned in the Nile River. He was weighed down by his golden armor.

Cleopatra moved to Rome to be with Julius Caesar. The people of Rome were angry because Julius Caesar already had a wife in Rome.

Some people in Rome thought that Julius Caesar was planning to unite Egypt and Rome and move the capital of Rome to Egypt! That angered many Romans. Therefore, two of Caesar's friends, Brutus and Cassius, decided to kill him. This was a hard decision for Brutus and Cassius, but they decided that Caesar must be killed to save Rome.

Brutus and Cassius murdered Caesar on March 15, 44 B.C. March 15 was the middle day of March. The Romans called March 15 the Ides of March.

Once again Cleopatra had to run for her life. The expression *"Beware the Ides of March"* now means to be careful!

Write T in front of the statements that are true and F in front of the statements that are false.

_____ 1. Cleopatra was queen while the pyramids were being built.

_____ 2. Cleopatra was married to her brother.

_____ 3. Julius Caesar was the ruler of the Roman Empire.

_____ 4. Ptolemy was killed in the war when he fell off of his horse.

_____ 5. The first day of March was called the Ides of March by the Romans.

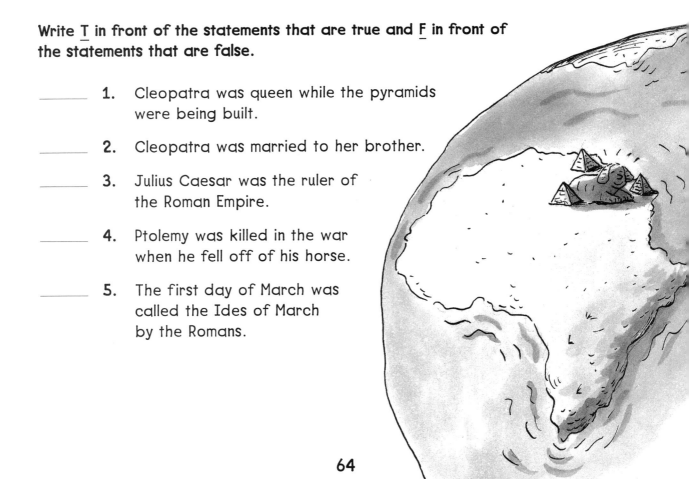

Write F if the statement below is a fact and O if the statement is an opinion.

_____ 1. Ptolemy was a better ruler than Julius Caesar.

_____ 2. Brutus and Cassius were evil men.

_____ 3. March 15 was called the Ides of March by the Romans.

_____ 4. Some Roman people were angry that Caesar brought Cleopatra to Rome.

Help Cleopatra arrange her jewels in the boxes.
Use the following clues to write the name of each
jewel on the box in the order that Cleopatra wants.

1. The Emerald Bracelet should be in the box that is the farthest left on this page.

2. The Onyx Pin should be in the center.

3. The Diamond Ring should be in the box directly to the right of the Onyx Pin.

4. The Pearl Choker should not be on the end.

Ruby   Diamond   Emerald   Onyx   Pearl
Crown   Ring   Bracelet   Pin   Choker

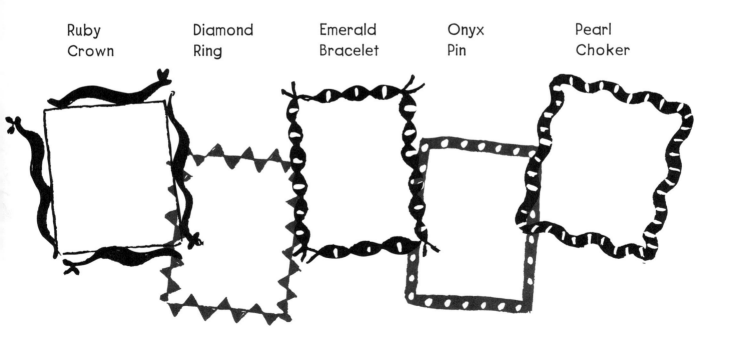

Frequent Flyer

Kidline Airlines is giving riders free tickets for travel up to 750 miles.
To get these free tickets, a rider must first travel 2500 miles on Kidline Airlines.
Use the information in the box to answer the problems below about Elena and
her travels. Show your work!

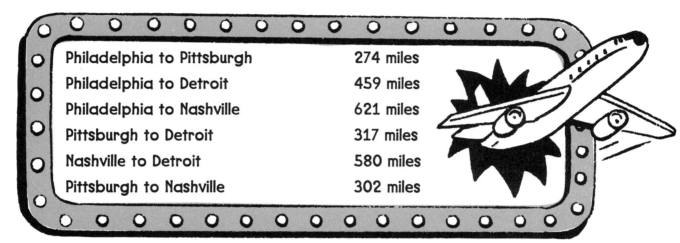

Philadelphia to Pittsburgh	274 miles
Philadelphia to Detroit	459 miles
Philadelphia to Nashville	621 miles
Pittsburgh to Detroit	317 miles
Nashville to Detroit	580 miles
Pittsburgh to Nashville	302 miles

1. Elena travels during her summer vacation.

   • She flies from Philadelphia to Pittsburgh to see her
     grandmother.

   • She flies from there to Nashville to visit a friend.

   • At the end of the week, she flies home (from Nashville to
     Philadelphia).

   How far does she fly altogether? _____

2. Elena's next opportunity to travel comes during July.

   • She flies from her home in Philadelphia to Detroit to visit
     her aunt and uncle.

   • They send her on a plane to Nashville
     to see country singers.

   • Elena flies back from Nashville to Detroit to spend
     another week with her aunt and uncle.

   How many miles has Elena flown this time? _____

3. Has Elena flown far enough this summer to get a free ticket? (Remember, you must fly 2500 miles on Kidline Airlines to get a free ticket.) _____

4. Can Elena use her free ticket to visit her aunt and uncle by flying from Philadelphia to Detroit, and then Detroit to Philadelphia? (Remember, you can only fly free up to 750 miles.) _____

If you were to win a free ticket to go anywhere in the United States, where would you go. Why? Make sure that you write an introductory sentence. Support that sentence with at least three good sentences to answer "why."

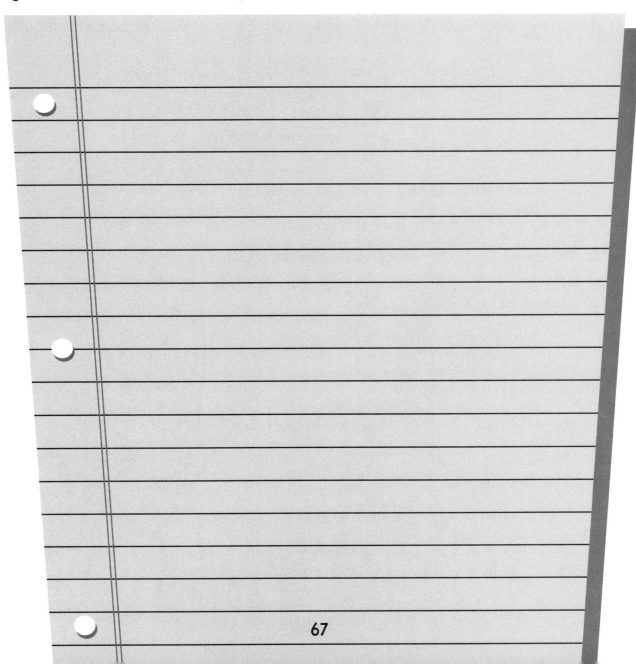

Helping Out

Fill in the blank with the correct helping verb from the box.

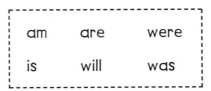

am	are	were
is	will	was

1. Today I _____ going to the movies with my friends.

2. Billy _____ eating his dinner now.

3. The children _____ have a picnic tomorrow.

4. I _____ walking to the park yesterday when I lost my way.

5. The Tigers _____ playing their baseball game now.

6. The Redskins _____ play their game tomorrow.

7. The Bulldogs _____ playing their game yesterday when it started to rain.

8. Tomorrow I _____ mow the lawn.

9. Today we _____ going to the Fourth of July fireworks.

Fill in the blank with either I or me.

1. Teddy and _____ like to play together.

2. "My father is taking Susan and _____ to the park," said Will.

3. My sister and _____ look like each other.

4. Jimmy, Robbie, and _____ are going to camp next week.

5. Sarah gave _____ a stick of gum.

6. Aunt Jane is giving _____ a present for my birthday.

Decimal Madness

Write the value of the underlined number.

1. 82.1<u>2</u>   _____ two hundredths _____
2. 3<u>0</u>7.09   _____
3. 63<u>8</u>.29   _____
4. 1000.0<u>1</u>   _____

Write these decimals in words.

1. 4.2   _____ four and two-tenths _____
2. 23.56   _____
3. 129.5   _____
4. 398.06   _____
5. 12.096   _____

Write as a decimal.

1. Six and fourteen hundredths   _____ 6.14 _____
2. One hundred and one tenth   _____
3. Two and seven one thousandths   _____
4. Twenty-nine and twenty-nine hundredths   _____
5. Twelve and thirteen hundredths   _____

Write these decimals in order from least to greatest.

1. 0.56, 0.61, 0.6   _____
2. 70.07, 70.70, 77.00, 70.77   _____
3. 45.6, 45.06, 45.5   _____
4. 6.8, 6.0, 6.3   _____

Write the decimal for these fractions.

1. $4\frac{3}{10}$ = __4.3__

2. $64\frac{8}{100}$ = _____

3. $128\frac{25}{100}$ = _____

4. $19\frac{4}{1000}$ = _____

5. $1\frac{1}{10}$ = _____

6. $27\frac{13}{100}$ = _____

Fill in the blank with > , < , or = .

1. 0.1 __>__ 0.01

2. 12.7 _____ 12.07

3. 135.1 _____ 135.9

4. 8.2 _____ 8.24

5. 4.00 _____ 4

6. 0.25 _____ 0.251

7. 1.67 _____ 2.00

Change to fractions.

1. 0.7 = $\frac{7}{10}$

2. 0.117 = _____

3. 0.18 = _____

4. 2.13 = _____

5. 8.2 = _____

6. 7.004 = _____

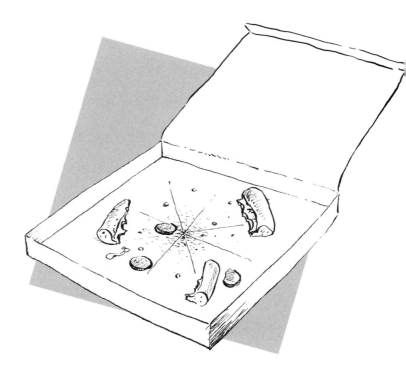

Write the sum or difference.

1. 7.7 + 2.9 = _____

2. 6.3 + 1.2 = _____

3. 9.2 - 0 = _____

4. 1.9 - 0.6 = _____

5. 6.1 - 3.8 = _____

6. 1.8 + 1.3 = _____

Solve.

1. John, Matt, and Sean each threw a basketball as far as they could. John threw the ball 7.6 yards, Matt threw it 10 yards, and Sean threw it 6.9 yards. Who threw it the farthest?

_____

2. The school is 2.3 miles from home. Mom drove us 1.8 miles and told us to walk the rest of the way. How far did we have to walk?

_____

3. On vacation we flew 107.9 kilometers and then drove 22.9 kilometers. How far did we travel?

_____

4. You need 12 ounces of chocolate for a recipe. The chocolate comes in bags of 9.5 ounces. Since you must buy 2 bags of chocolate, how much extra chocolate will you have?

_____

71

Dear Teacher

Write a letter to your fourth grade teacher. Tell your teacher what you liked best about third grade. Then tell what was the hardest part of third grade. Finally, tell your fourth grade teacher what you are looking forward to in fourth grade.

Dear Fourth Grade Teacher,

_____

_____

_____

_____

_____

_____

_____

_____

_____

_____

_____

_____

_____

_____

_____

Signed,

_____

Your name

BOOK SECTION

The book section provides worksheets for five books.
Three are chosen; the last two are free choice.

Summer Wheels by Eve Bunting

Bunnicula by Deborah and James Howe

Catwings by Ursula K. Le Guin

Summer Wheels

Read *Summer Wheels* by Eve Bunting. Then use complete sentences to answer these questions about the story.

Chapter One

1. What does the Bicycle Man do with the bikes he fixes?

   _____

   _____

2. What does the Bicycle Man mean when he says, "Early Birds get the best

   bikes"? _____

   _____

3. What two things does the Bicycle Man tell the children when

   they take out a bike? _____

   _____

4. At the beginning of the book, what does Lawrence think

   the Bicycle Man loves more than anything? _____

   _____

Chapter Two

1. Where do Lawrence and Brady put their bikes when they

   return? Why? _____

   _____

   _____

2. Which bike does the new guy pick? _____

3. Why do you think the new guy writes his name as "Abrehem

   Lincoln"? _____

   _____

Chapter Three

1. Why is Lawrence "madder than mad"? _____

   _____

2. What does Lawrence decide to do instead of going to the

   park as usual? _____

3. Why do you think the Bicycle Man is not angry at "Abrehem

   Lincoln"? _____

   _____

Chapter Four

Circle the best answer to the questions.

1. What reason did the new guy give for not bringing back the bike?

   a. He lost the bike.

   b. He said that anyone who was dumb enough to give it for
      free deserved to lose it.

   c. He couldn't remember the way back.

2. What is the Bicycle Man's rule about broken bikes?

   a. If you break a bike, you can't take out another.

   b. Just bring the bike back and the Bicycle Man will fix it.

   c. If a bike breaks while you have it, you have to fix it.

3. Do you think the Bicycle Man was foolish to let the new guy take another bike? Why or why not? _____

_____

4. What name does the new guy sign in the book this time? _____

_____

Chapter Five

The new guy does not return the second bike. What do the boys do? Number these sentences 1 through 5 to show the order in which they happened.

_____ Lawrence and Brady go to find the new guy.

_____ They see the new guy riding the broken bike down steps.

_____ Lawrence and Brady tell the new guy to return the bike.

_____ The new guy returns with Lawrence and Brady to the Man.

_____ Lawrence and Brady see a big bunch of kids.

Chapter Six

1. The new guy brings his broken bike back to the Bicycle Man. What does he know he must do? _____

_____

2. At the end of this chapter, what does Lawrence think the Bicycle Man likes even more than his bikes? _____

_____

3. What did you think of the book? _____

_____

The story in *Summer Wheels* is told by Lawrence. Everything that happens is told from his point of view. What if the story were told from the point of view of the new guy? How would he describe what happened? On the lines below, write a new version of the story in which the new guy tells the story.

_____

_____

_____

_____

_____

_____

_____

_____

_____

_____

_____

_____

_____

_____

_____

_____

_____

_____

BUNNICULA

Find a cozy place to read *Bunnicula*, by Deborah and James Howe. Don't forget to read the Editor's Note in the beginning of this Rabbit-Tale of Mystery!

Where does the Editor's Note say the author got the book?

_____

_____

_____

Chapter One

In Chapter 1, we find that a family, whose last name was _____,

had gone to the movies. The movie they had seen was about _____.

Waiting at home for the family was the family dog named _____ and

the family cat named _____.

While at the movies, the family found _____ on Toby's chair. A

note was also found. Harold determined that the note was written in a Russian

dialect that said, "_____

_____." The family decided to name the new

pet _____ since they found him at a Dracula movie.

Chapter Two

Chester had one thing that he loved to do after the family went to sleep. He

loved to _____. Therefore he had quite a good imagination.

Chester told Harold two strange things about Bunnicula. First, he noted that the

bunny's fur made it look like Bunnicula was wearing a _____.

Second, he said that instead of buck teeth, Bunnicula had _____.

Chapter Three

Bunnicula sleeps all day and stays awake at night. _____ now stays

awake at night to watch Bunnicula. Chester told Harold that one night, while

watching Bunnicula, he fell asleep because he was watching a _____

on the clock. When he woke up, the bunny's cage was _____. The

next morning, Mr. Monroe found a _____ in the refrigerator. Chester

thinks that Bunnicula caused the tomato to turn white because Bunnicula is a

_____!

Chapter Four

Chester read his books and studied Bunnicula. He then found that the lettuce and

carrots in Bunnicula's cage had _____. He believes that Bunnicula

turns the vegetables white by _____. The chapter ends with Chester

and Harold finding a white _____.

Chapter Five

Chapter 5 opens with the Monroe family upset because all the vegetables in the

refrigerator were _____. Chester took matters into his own hands.

He took Mr. Monroe's _____ and draped it across his back like a cape. He made a strange face. When Mr. Monroe reached for him, Chester flipped onto his back. He was pretending to be a _____. He actually bit _____ on the neck! The Monroes did not understand at all. They thought that he was cold and put him into his bright yellow _____. Harold told Chester to stand outside Bunnicula's cage in that silly sweater and Bunnicula would laugh himself to death!

Chapter Six

This funny chapter tells us that Chester read a book called *The Mark of the Vampire*. That book told him that if one wore _____ around his neck, a vampire would not be able to move. Since Harold could not stand the smell, he slept outside. When he came inside, Chester was yelling his head off because _____. As soon as the Monroes went to work, Chester unlocked Bunnicula's cage and asked Harold to carry out the sleeping bunny. He had read his book and found that to destroy a vampire it is necessary to pound a _____ into the heart of a vampire. Unfortunately, instead of a "stake," or stick, Chester got the family's dinner _____! Just when things were getting nasty, Chester stopped because _____.

Chapter Seven

In Chapter 7 we find that Chester has a new plan: _____. Harold was furious because he liked Bunnicula.

Chapter Eight

Harold decided to save Bunnicula, so he went into Bunnicula's cage and carried

him _____. Chester discovered Harold's plan. We almost had a sad

ending. However, Harold _____. Because of that, the Monroes came

running into the room to stop the trouble.

Chapter Nine

Harold was very unhappy because Bunnicula was his new friend and Chester was

his old friend. He did not want either one to get hurt. The animals were taken to

the _____. He told the Monroes that Bunnicula's problem was

_____ and Chester's problem was _____.

Do you think that Bunnicula was a vampire bunny? Or do you think Chester's

imagination got the best of him? Why?

_____

_____

_____

Write a few sentences telling about a time that you or someone you know was

really scared, but when things were sorted out, you found that the situation

was not really scary: the imagination had run wild!

_____

_____

_____

Catwings

Read *Catwings* by Ursula K. Le Guin.

Chapter 1

Circle the best answer to each question.

1. What was so special about Mrs. Jane Tabby's kittens?
   a. They were beautiful, well brought up children.
   b. They had wings.
   c. Their father was a "fly-by-night."

2. Why did Mrs. Tabby worry about her children?
   a. The sparrows had moved away.
   b. The children could not fly very well.
   c. The neighborhood was terrible and getting worse.

3. What did Mrs. Tabby understand when the huge dog chased little Harriet?
   a. The children could fly well.
   b. The children were born with wings so they could fly from the neighborhood.
   c. The children needed a good dinner.

Draw a picture of Thelma, Roger, James, and Harriet flying from the neighborhood.

Chapter 2

Circle the best meaning for the underlined word.

1. The pigeon <u>peered</u> at the kittens.
    smiled   pulled   looked carefully

2. James <u>muttered</u> that pigeons are dumb.
    coughed   mumbled   laughed

3. The kittens <u>gazed</u> westward toward the city.
    stared   marched   shouted

4. The kittens beat their wings hard to keep their bodies
    <u>aloft</u>.
    joined   hidden   up in the air

5. The kittens let the wind <u>bear</u> them up.
    sing   hold   join

6. The kittens <u>descended</u> slowly from the air.
    came down went up   flew sideways

7. Roger <u>crouched</u> on the bank of the stream.
    ran   stood   laid close to the ground

Chapter 3

Circle the best answer to each question.

1. Why were the birds upset?
    a. They did not like cats.
    b. They were worried about the safety of their babies.
    c. The birds could not fly as well as the cats.

2. What did Owl finally understand?
    a. The cats would be good friends.
    b. The baby birds would have to learn to
    take care of themselves.
    c. The cats could not be allowed to harm
    the baby birds.

3. What did the cats learn from Owl's attacks on Roger and James?
   a. Owls are smart birds.
   b. They learned how the birds felt when they were threatened.
   c. Cats could not fly as well as birds.

4. Who were the Shoes and the Hands that the kittens remembered?

   _____

5. Harriet saw A Hands. Why does she think this one is the right kind?

   _____

Chapter 4

Draw a line from the cause (the reason) to its effect (its result).

1. Hank had not seen the cats.	Thelma was not afraid of Susan.
2. The children put out food for the cats.	The cats wanted Susan and Hank to make a home for them.
3. Susan did not try to catch Thelma.	The cats ate the food and trusted the children.
4. Hank gently stroked Roger between the wings.	The other cats wanted Hank and Susan to pet them.
5. Susan and Hank were kind to the cats.	Hank did not believe in flying cats.

Not Just for Kids

Some of the most famous books written are picture books.
Picture books are loved by young and old alike. Choose a
picture book that you loved as a young child. Or, find one that
a young friend or brother or sister suggests. Try reading that
book aloud, perhaps to that friend, brother, or sister.

1. What is the title of your picture book?

   _____

   _____

2. Who is the author? _____

3. You will find that the vocabulary (the words used by the
   author) is often not easy in a picture book. Name three of
   the hardest words in the book and tell what they mean. Use
   a dictionary if necessary.

   _____

   _____

   _____

   _____

   _____

4. Picture books are important because of their pictures. Who illustrated your book?

_____

_____

5. Describe the kind of pictures in your book. Are they black and white, color, fantasy, childlike, or detailed?

_____

_____

_____

6. What makes you like this book? _____

_____

_____

_____

7. If you were to write a book for children, what would you write about?

_____

_____

_____

_____

_____

_____

_____

_____

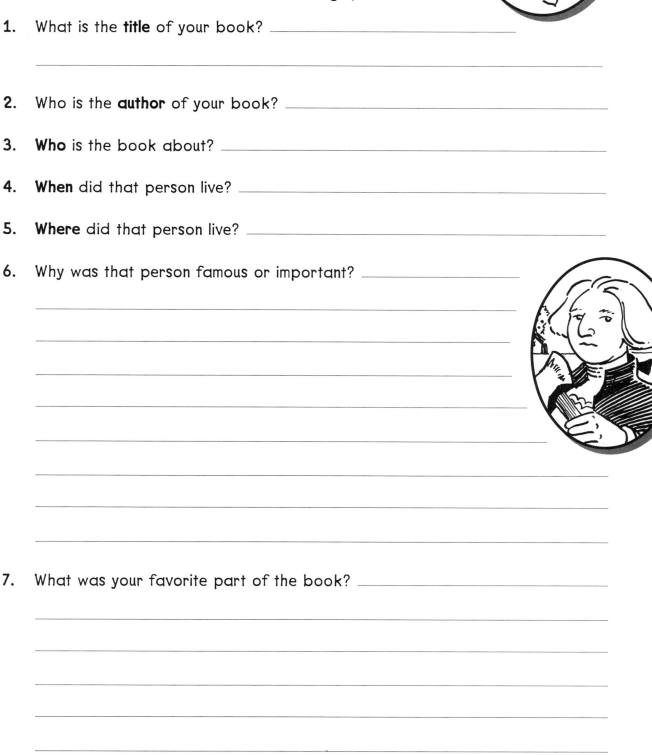

Biography

Find a book that is a true story about someone's life.
Read the book and then answer the following questions:

1. What is the **title** of your book? _____

   _____

2. Who is the **author** of your book? _____

3. **Who** is the book about? _____

4. **When** did that person live? _____

5. **Where** did that person live? _____

6. Why was that person famous or important? _____

   _____

   _____

   _____

   _____

   _____

   _____

   _____

7. What was your favorite part of the book? _____

   _____

   _____

   _____

   _____

   _____

8. How are YOU like the person in your book? Think of at least two things.

_____
_____
_____
_____
_____
_____
_____
_____

9. What else would you like to know about the person in your biography?

_____
_____
_____
_____
_____
_____
_____
_____

10. If you were to write a biography today, who would you write about? Why?

_____
_____
_____

Answer Key

PAGE 5
1. 816
2. 5406
3. 6042
4. 6001
5. 2006

1. 1500
2. 355
3. 8500
4. 45
5. 250

1. two hundred twenty
2. one thousand sixty-seven
3. seven thousand seven hundred seventy-seven
4. six hundred one
5. eight thousand four hundred ninety-six

PAGE 6
1. 8000
2. 8
3. 800

1. 40
2. 40,000
3. 40
4. 400

1. V
2. IV
3. IX
4. XXV
5. XXXIX

1. 8
2. 34
3. 19
4. 27

99; 887; 6987; 34,546; 300,000

8 pieces of candy

PAGE 7
Sentences will vary.
1. F I went down all the easy hills.
2. F We stopped in every snack bar.
3. S Lauren never fell all day.
4. S Ski slopes are most crowded on holidays.
5. F Beginners are not allowed down the hardest slopes.
6. F Don't walk under the ski lift.
7. S My brother won the ski race.

PAGE 8
1. My ski club goes to Jack Frost Mountain every Tuesday evening. It is so much fun.
2. I take lessons every year. You can never practice too much.
3. Snowboarding looks so cool! If you want to learn to snowboard, start on easy mountains.

1. The youngest skier
2. My father
3. The yellow ski hat
4. People who ski
5. you
6. These mittens

PAGE 9

X	4	3	7	1	8	10	6	5	2	9
5	20	15	35	5	40	50	30	25	10	45
8	32	24	56	8	64	80	48	40	16	72
10	40	30	70	10	80	100	60	30	20	90
4	16	12	28	4	32	40	24	20	8	36
7	28	21	49	7	56	70	42	35	14	63
9	36	27	63	9	72	90	54	45	18	81
1	4	3	7	1	8	10	6	5	2	9
6	24	18	42	6	48	60	36	30	12	54
3	12	9	21	3	24	30	18	15	6	27
2	8	6	14	2	16	20	12	10	4	18

PAGE 11
1. T 2. T 3. T 4. F 5. T 6. F

1. pink
2. flowers
3. vegetables
4. birds
5. toes

PAGE 12
1. colonies
2. echoes
3. colors
4. muscles
5. roosts
6. bodies

1. F 2. O 3. F 4. O 5. F 6. O

1. mammal—animal that feeds its young with milk
2. nocturnal—active at night
3. colony—a group of animals that live together
4. roost—homesite
5. echolocation—locating objects with echoes
6. climate—the regular weather in an area
7. wingspan—measurement from tip of one wing to tip of other

PAGE 13
1. 9 weeks
2. row 2: 9, 5, 1; row 3: 2
3. P.M.
4. P.M.
5. A.M.

PAGE 15
1. 70
2. 120
3. 80
4. 250
5. 4910
6. 6790

1. 300
2. 600
3. 100
4. 200
5. 3000
6. 7500

1. 7000
2. 3000
3. 4000
4. 7000
5. 1000
6. 5000

PAGE 16
1. across
2. lost
3. story
4. Where
5. thought
6. until
7. been
8. might
9. usually
10. people
11. family
12. answer
13. picture
14. through
15. toward
16. light
17. enough
18. several

PAGE 17
1. $\frac{4}{6}$ or $\frac{2}{3}$
2. $\frac{6}{10}$ or $\frac{3}{5}$
3. $\frac{7}{12}$
4. $\frac{4}{5}$
5. $\frac{5}{8}$
6. $\frac{4}{7}$
7. $\frac{5}{6}$
8. $\frac{5}{9}$

PAGE 18
1. b 2. c 3. a 4. b

1. We went to the beach in August.
2. Did you go at all this summer?
3. If you went to the beach, raise your hand. X
4. Are you sure it was the beach and not the mountains?
5. Be honest! X
6. I hope we go to the beach every year.

1. John
2. Camp Archbald
3. The sports

PAGE 19
1. b 2. a 3. c

1. miles
2. driving
3. lunches
4. boxes
5. sleeping
6. paved

PAGE 20
1. 863
2. 409
3. 333
4. 414
5. 642
6. 545
7. 3402

PAGES 23–24

1. Poseidon—a pearl necklace
2. Athene—taught her to use a spinning wheel
3. Hera—curiosity
4. Demeter—taught her to garden
5. Aphrodite—beauty
6. Apollo—taught her to love music
7. Zeus—a lovely, golden box

1. The people did not appreciate what the gods had done.
2. Zeus told Pandora never to open the golden box.
3. She could not stop wondering what was in the golden box.
4. Pandora tried hiding the box in a closet.
5. They were the creatures of unhappiness: Disease, Cruelty, Hatred, War, Pain, and Sorrow.
6. A beautiful, fragrant flower rose up.
7. The person might mean that you will find trouble.

1. Pandora
2. Pandora was very curious.
3. a shiny metal object
4. With bad, there is often good.

PAGE 26

The answers go clockwise from the top.

1. 9, 5, 7, 1, 11, 6
2. 4, 1, 9, 5, 12, 3, 7, 2
3. 8, 2, 4, 6, 9, 7, 10, 3
4. 4, 9, 8, 5, 2, 6, 3, 7

PAGE 27

1. August 5
2. August 2, 7
3. August 1, 3, 6
4. $1.50; $1.00
5. 160
6. $16.00

PAGES 28–29

1. Sample answers: knife, knight
2. globe
3. 100
4. Philadelphia
5. 7
6. Florida
7. Maine
8. a, e, i, o, u, y
9. consonant
10. 90
11. midnight
12. star
13. 60
14. 24
15. vibration
16. friction
17. Answers will vary
18. 3
19. February
20. George Washington
21. hive
22. Sample answer: kangaroo
23. gas
24. 1/2
25. iceberg
26. 5
27. 100
28. fish
29. 18
30. electric
31. Saturn
32. 2

PAGE 30

1. 7   2. 3   3. 5   4. 1   5. 4   6. 6   7. 2

PAGE 31

10's: 1430, 6730, 980, 2950, 3050, 6670
100's: 1400, 6700, 1000, 3000, 3100, 6700
1000's: 1000, 7000, 1000, 3000, 3000, 7000

1. 4   6. 9   10. 9   14. 7   18. 3
2. 6   7. 9   11. 8   15. 6   19. 9
3. 5   8. 0   12. 8   16. 10   20. 7
4. 8   9. 7   13. 7   17. 9   21. 11
5. 6

PAGE 32

Answers are given clockwise from top.

1. 35, 63, 42, 56, 14, 49
2. 48, 36, 12, 54, 42, 24, 18, 30
3. 72, 40, 8, 56, 16, 32, 64, 48
4. 243   7. 552   10. 162
5. 190   8. 292   11. 846
6. 282   9. 602

PAGE 33

1. 30
2. you
3. 10 books more
4. Christopher and Jamell
5. 55 books
6. 85 books

PAGE 34

1. rode
2. whole
3. knows
4. buy
5. sun
6. Knights

PAGE 35

7:00 8:15 9:05 9:45
8:30 10:45 10:20 11:00
Theater 1   1 hour 30 minutes
Theater 2   2 hours 30 minutes
Theater 3   1 hour 15 minutes
Theater 4   1 hour 15 minutes

PAGE 36

1. gallon   2. cup   3. quart

1. 8 cups   4. 16 quarts   6. 12 cups; 3 quarts
2. 12 quarts 5. 16 cups   7. 16 cups; 4 quarts
3. 4 cups

PAGE 40

1. mirrors
2. The Hubble Space Telescope is in space.
3. Discovery
4. Endeavor

1. F   2. F   3. F   4. T   5. T   6. F

PAGE 41

1. F   2. O   3. O   4. F

c. telescope   f. blur   b. image
e. invention   a. precise   d. intense

PAGE 44

1. 7 days
2. April, June, September, November
3. January, March, May, July, August, October, December
4. February, 28 or 29
5. 365 or 366
6. Thursday
7. February, Friday, Sunday; Tuesday, October, August
8. Jan., Sat., Mon., Sept., Wed., Dec.

PAGE 45

1. 4, 6   4. 3, 2   7. 2154   10. 342
2. 5, 4   5. 8, 6, 8 8. 4576   Bonus: 938
3. 0, 2   6. 9, 9   9. 3560

PAGES 48–49

1. Lady Liberty
2. Frédéric Auguste Bartholdi
3. France
4. the love of liberty
5. People get their first view of the new world in New York harbor.
6. France paid for the statue.
7. America paid for the pedestal.
8. the statue's arm and torch
9. the copper head
10. October 28, 1886
11. 11 years

1. torch—light to welcome people to America
2. tablet—Independence Day
3. crown with 7 rays—liberty spreading across 7 seas
4. broken chain—freedom from England

PAGE 50

3 recognize   1 liberty   4 crate
7 statue   8 pedestal   5 harbor
10 immigrant   6 centennial 9 fundraising
2 symbol

1. F   2. O   3. F   4. O   5. F   6. F

PAGE 52
1. flowers   2. bike   3. man   4. children
1. sink   2. boy   3. mother   4. bird
1. boys   2. children   3. people   4. dogs
1. aunt's   2. uncles'   3. players'   4. children's

PAGE 53
1. capital   2. names   3. city   4. holidays
1. Labor Day 2. Emily   3. England 4. Colorado River
1. lady's   2. watchs   3. wifes   4. valleyes

PAGE 55
1. 4:30 P.M.   3. $4,605.00
2. 223 students   4. 18 pounds

PAGE 57
1. $2.81, $2.19   3. $5.27
2. no, $1.88   4. yes

PAGES 58–59
1. $.54   4. $69.76   7. 961   10. 329 r. 3
2. $15.44   5. $57.90   8. 481   11. 999 r. 2
3. $19.18   6. $17.30   9. 256   12. 513 r. 2

1. 9 boxes   3. $39.00   5. 18 friends
2. 42 pages   4. 8 bushes   6. 21 cupcakes

1. 1   3. 4   5. 7   7. 654
2. 0   4. 27   6. 0   8. 8

$6 \times 8 = 48$ $48 \div 6 = 8$ $48 \div 8 = 6$

PAGE 60
1. Michael lives at 23 Poplar Street.
2. Did Amy visit the Parkland Zoo?
3. Ted has visited both the Atlantic Ocean and the Pacific Ocean.
4. My grandmother and Aunt Barbara live in Carson City, Kansas.
5. Lauren goes to Fourth Street Elementary School.
6. Have you ever visited New York City?

1. to   3. to, too   5. two, to, to
2. two   4. too, to

PAGE 61
1. $\frac{6}{8}$ or $\frac{3}{4}$ 2. $\frac{3}{12}$ or $\frac{1}{4}$ 3. $\frac{20}{55}$ or $\frac{4}{11}$ 4. $\frac{17}{100}$

1. $3\frac{1}{3}$ 3. $4\frac{1}{2}$ 5. $1\frac{2}{24}$ or $1\frac{1}{12}$ 7. $2\frac{2}{3}$
2. $3\frac{1}{7}$ 4. $1\frac{1}{4}$ 6. $7\frac{2}{10}$ or $7\frac{1}{5}$ 8. $1\frac{1}{6}$

1. $\frac{7}{4}$ 3. $\frac{46}{7}$ 5. $\frac{21}{9}$ 7. $\frac{47}{6}$
2. $\frac{53}{10}$ 4. $\frac{74}{9}$ 6. $\frac{58}{7}$ 8. $\frac{12}{5}$

PAGE 62
1. $\frac{6}{20}, \frac{1}{2}, \frac{4}{5}$ 2. $\frac{1}{4}, \frac{1}{2}, \frac{3}{4}, \frac{7}{8}$ 3. $\frac{2}{18}, \frac{1}{6}, \frac{4}{9}, \frac{2}{3}$

1. 27 minutes   3. 33,472   5. 14,616
2. 8 fish   4. 3366

PAGE 64
1. F   2. T   3. T   4. F   5. F

PAGE 65
1. O   2. O   3. F   4. F

emerald bracelet, pearl choker, onyx pin, diamond ring, ruby crown

PAGES 66–67
1. 1197 miles   2. 1619 miles   3. yes   4. no

PAGE 68
1. am   4. was   6. will   8. will
2. is   5. are   7. were   9. are
3. will

1. I   2. me   3. I   4. I   5. me   6. me

PAGE 69
2. no tens   3. eight ones   4. one hundredth

2. twenty-three and fifty-six hundredths
3. one hundred twenty-nine and five tenths
4. three hundred ninety-eight and six hundredths
5. twelve and ninety-six thousandths

2. 100.1
3. 2.007
4. 29.29
5. 12.13

1. 0.56, 0.6, 0.61
2. 70.07, 70.70, 70.77, 77.00
3. 45.06, 45.5, 45.6
4. 6.0, 6.3, 6.8

PAGE 70
2. 64.08   4. 19.004   6. 27.13
3. 128.25   5. 1.1
2. >   3. <   4. <   5. =   6. <   7. <
2. 117/1000   4. 2 13/100   6. 7 4/1000
3. 18/100   5. 8 2/10

PAGE 71
1. 10.6   3. 9.2   5. 2.3
2. 7.5   4. 1.3   6. 3.1

1. Matt   2. .5 miles   3. 130.8 kilometers   4. 7 ounces

PAGES 74–76

Chapter One
1. He lets the neighborhood kids use them for free.
2. The kids who get there early get the best pick of the bikes.
3. He tells them to have the bikes back by four o'clock and to ride safely.
4. He thinks the Bicycle Man loves bikes more than anything.

Chapter Two
1. They put them against the far corner wall. They do not want other kids to pick their bikes.
2. The new guy chooses the bike Lawrence was riding.
3. Possible answer: The new guy may be thinking about keeping the bike.

Chapter Three
1. He is mad because the new guy did not return the bike.
2. He decides to go find the new guy.
3. Possible answer: He cares more about the kids than about the bikes.

Chapter Four
1. b. He said that anyone who was dumb enough to give it for free deserved to lose it.
2. c. If a bike breaks while you have it, you have to fix it.
3. Answers will vary.
4. He signs Abrehem Lincin.

Chapter Five

1. Lawrence and Brady go to find the new guy.
3. They see the new guy riding the broken bike down steps.
4. Lawrence and Brady tell the new guy to return the bike.
5. The new guy returns with Lawrence and Brady to the Man.
2. Lawrence and Brady see a big bunch of kids.

Chapter Six

1. He knows that he must fix it.
2. Lawrence thinks the Bicycle Man likes kids even more than bikes.
3. Answers will vary.

PAGES 78–81

A dog named Harold brought it to him.

Chapter 1: Monroe, Dracula, Harold, Chester, a rabbit, Take good care of my baby, Bunnicula
Chapter 2: read books, cape, fangs
Chapter 3: Chester, pendulum, empty, white tomato, vampire
Chapter 4: turned white, sucking out all the juices, zucchini
Chapter 5: white, towel, vampire, Harold, sweater
Chapter 6: garlic, Mrs. Monroe was giving him a bath, stake, steak, the Monroes returned home
Chapter 7: Chester is starving Bunnicula
Chapter 8: to a bowl of salad, barked
Chapter 9: veterinarian, extreme hunger, he was emotionally overwrought

PAGES 82–84

Chapter One
1. b. They had wings.
2. c. The neighborhood was terrible and getting worse.
3. b. The children were born with wings so they could fly from the neighborhood.

Chapter Two
1. looked carefully
2. mumbled   3. stared
4. up in the air
5. hold
6. came down
7. laid close to the ground

Chapter Three
1. b. They were worried about the safety of their babies.
2. c. The cats could not be allowed to harm the baby birds.
3. b. They learned how the birds felt when they were threatened.
4. They belonged to the people in the city who picked the cats up.
5. It brought her food and did not try to touch her.

Chapter Four
1. Hank had not seen the cats. — Hank did not believe in flying cats.
2. The children put out food for the cats. — The cats ate the food and trusted the children.
3. Susan did not try to catch Thelma. — Thelma was not afraid of Susan.
4. Hank gently stroked Roger between the wings. — The other cats wanted Hank and Susan to pet them.
5. Susan and Hank were kind to the cats. — The cats wanted Susan and Hank to make a home for them.